Samuel Jenks

Diary of Captain Samuel Jenks During the French and Indian

war 1760

Samuel Jenks

Diary of Captain Samuel Jenks During the French and Indian war 1760

ISBN/EAN: 9783337015152

Printed in Europe, USA, Canada, Australia, Japan

Cover: Foto ©ninafisch / pixelio.de

More available books at **www.hansebooks.com**

JOURNAL OF CAPTAIN SAMUEL JENKS.

AT a meeting of the MASSACHUSETTS HISTORICAL SOCIETY, held March 13, 1890, the Rev. HENRY F. JENKS communicated a diary kept in 1760, during the French and Indian War, by his great-grandfather, Capt. Samuel Jenks, which covers the same period as the diary of Sergeant David Holden, already printed by the Society.[1]

Samuel Jenks was born in Lynn, Mass., March 12, 1732. He learned his trade (that of a blacksmith) from his father, and wrought at it successively in Chelsea (on Point Shirley), — where the journal following shows that he was residing in 1760, when he started on the campaign which it records, — and in Medford, Newton, — where his son William (H. C. 1797, and member of our Society for many years) was born, — and in Boston. In the " Boston Directory " of 1789, the first published, his name appears, — " Jenks, Samuel and Son, black-smiths and bellows makers, at the sign of the bellows, Gardner's Wharf, Ann Street "; and in that of 1796, which appears to have been the next one published, his residence is given on Cross Street, where he was known to have been living in 1787, when the same son entered the Boston Latin School. He died at Cambridge, June 8, 1801.

" He was twice," says his son,[2] " engaged in military expeditions, being in the Canadian campaigns of 1758 and 1760, in the latter of which he was the youngest captain in the

---

[1] See 2 Proceedings, vol. iv. pp. 384-409.
[2] N. E. Hist. Gen. Reg., vol. ix., July, 1855.

provincial army; and the late Governor Brooks assured me that the instruction which he derived at Medford from my father's experience and military knowledge was of essential service to himself at the opening of the Revolutionary contest."

In the " Mercury and New-England Palladium," of Friday, June 12, 1801, was published the following obituary : —

" Died at Cambridge, on Monday, Samuel Jenks, Esq., aged 70, late of this town, a captain of the provincial service of 1760, and an active officer in the campaign of 1758. In the character of this upright and worthy man were combined those qualities which render piety amiable and virtue engaging. His mind was enlightened and candid. The leisure of a laborious and useful life was employed in furnishing it with various information. Convinced of the truth and importance of the Gospel, he was a rational, sincere, and practical Christian, and experienced in the closing scenes of life that peace of mind and hope of future happiness which it alone can confer. — As a friend, a brother, a husband, and a father, he was tender and affectionate. As a citizen, he was blameless, and governed his whole conduct by the strictest rules of equity. He was a lover of order and good government, and an ardent friend to his country. To society he has bequeathed an exemplary pattern of honesty, integrity, and Christian meekness ; to his children a rich legacy, — the inestimable treasure of an unblemished reputation."

He was buried in Saugus, and his gravestone is but a few steps from the gate in the burying-ground.

Samuel Jenks, his Journall of the Campaign in 1760.

Point Shirley, May the 22ᵈ, 1760. Then set out on a campaign for the total reduction of Canada.

Wednsday, 28ᵗʰ *of May.* Arivd at Albany to the camp; found my company incamping in good health.

Thirsday, 29. Sent a letter home by the post. Recᵈ orders to be ready for command up the river & to leave my tent standing.

Fryday, 30ᵗʰ *of May.* Rec'd orders from Genrall Amherst to proceed to Fort Miller with a number of battoes loaded with provisions & a com'd of 50 men.

Monday, June 2ᵈ, 1760. Onloade the battoes at the rifts above half moon, & proceed with emty battoes to Still Water.

Tuseday, 3ᵈ *June.* Recᵈ 240 barrells flour & drew 2 days allowance to carry to Fort Miller.

Wednsday, 4ᵗʰ *June.* Arivᵈ at Fort Miller at night & landed the provisions, & am here stationed for the transportation of provisions from hence to Fort Edward.

Thirsday, 5th. Drew five days allowance to bring my men up to the time of others on station draw.

Fryday, 6th *of June*. Capt Smith ariv^d to releive me & for me to proceed forward with my own company. This day prou^d wet, & a sorry party of the Massachusetts troops ariv^d. We were hurried in transporting the provisions & battoes across the carrying place.

Saturday, 7th. Continued at ye station in giting over battoes & provisions.

Sunday, 8th. Orders for my company to proceed with the party that is ready for Fort Edward; myself to tary till Col^o Th^{os} arives for my orders to proceed. This day my company put of in battoes for Fort Edward, & I have rec^d orders to follow them in the first boats.

Monday, June 9th. Imbarqu^d on board Capt. Dunbars battoe for Fort Edward; ariv^d there before night; found my company incamp^t on the plain: went to view the fort, which I think is well built, but not well sictuated for to stand a seige.

Tuseday, 10th. Rec^d orders to march to Lake George, & march^t of about 10 oclock A. M. in one colum. Ariv^d at Lake George, & incamp^t before night.

Wednsday, 11 *June*. Remaind incamp^t; went to view the works; drew 2 days allowance to carry us to Ticondaroga.

Thirsday, 12 *June*. Sent a letter home by Mr Dix. . . . This morning struck our tents, & decamp^t at revaloe beating, then march^t down to ye battoes & imbarqu^d for Ticondaroga. The wind blowing hard a head, we put a shore at a small distance from ye fort on ye east side ye lake; the wind abateing, we set off & came to the first narrows on a small island & stopt to cook, haveing come 12 miles. The land on each side is exceeding mountainous, & abounds with vast number of rattlesnakes; our people kill^d 6 or 8 on this small island. Then put of, as soon as the rear came up & refresh^t themselves, to another island near Sabbath Day Point, & campt.

Fryday, 13th *June*. We got our breakfasts; then the Col^o gave orders to put off for Ticondaroga. Got there about three oclock P. M. & landed, & the Col^o went with a small escort to the fort & return^d; gave orders for the troops to march & incamp at the saw mill about a mile from ye landing, which was accordingly done; here all the officers that had never been on this land had to pay their entrance.

Saturday, 14th *June*. Remaind incampt at the mills. Here great numbers of the camp ladys came down from Crown Point on their way to Albany; sum of them interceding to be taken back. Here we are like to draw arms, haveing marcht all the way hither without. Expect to march for Crown Point to morrow, having detacht Lieut.

Pope & 12 men to tarry at Ticondaroga with L.! Col? Miller, who has a detachment of 300 men to stop there.

Sunday, 15th *June.* This morning we drew our arms & six cartriges a man. After delivering out the arms & ammunitision we imbarqu[d] on board battoes, 32 in each, for Crownpoint; set off, & pas[d] by the fort at Ticondaroga, which is very pleasantly scituated on y[e] Lake Champlain, & commands the Narrows and the entrance of South Bay. Here lay the Great Reddoe & 2 sloops waiting for a wind to proceed to Crown-point. It being late in the day, we could not reach Crownpoint. The Col? ordered the regiment to incamp near a block house, which is 2 miles from the main fort. The land on each side this lake is level, & looks like good land, & all looks pleasant & agreable.

Monday, 16th *June.* Decamp[t] early this morning, & arivd at Crownpoint; landed above the fort, & incampt. This day it raind & thundred prety much in y[e] forenoon. Went to view the works, which I think, when finished, may be justly stil[d] the strongest place the English has on the continent. Here, I[;]bleive, is our station for this campeign, for there is an immense sight of work to be done before these forts are compleated.

Tuseday, 17th *June.* This morning I was ordred off with 200 men across the lake in order to git sum spruce. Cap[t] Brewer of the Rangers went to pilot us; when we got a shore we march[t] with front, rear, & flank guards. Return[d] without any molestation from y[e] enemy; brought a fine quantity of spruce. The commanding officer on the station gave us his thanks for the service we had done.

Wednesday, 18th *June.* This day I was off duty. At the evening we espy[d] a fire [1] made on the west side the lake about 6 miles down. Imediately a party & sum of our pequit gaurd was sent in 2 battoes & a whale boat for to discover who they be. As Rogers is out with a large party tis supposed it is sum of his returning.

Thirsday, 19 *June.* This day, Major Skeen, who went out to se wat the fire was made for, returned about 9 oclock A. M., & brought in 2 of our men that run away from the French; they had been without provisions 6 day, living on strawberrys & roots. About noon we discover[d] several boats coming up the lake from toward St Johns, which proves to be sum of our people that have been in captivity; there is about 130 in all. They bring us the agreable news of the French being obliged to raise the seige of Quebeck in the greatest confusion, with the loss of 3,500 men, & all their arteliry, & all their camp equipage, & that the country is all in confusion.

Fryday, 20 *June.* This day the train are carying the shott & shells

---

[1] See Sergeant Holden's Journal, 2 Proceedings, vol. iv. p. 302.

in great numbers out of the fort down to the wharfe, in order to ship on board the vessels; & great numbers are at work in preparing cartriges & other necessarys for the expedition which I bleive will be form^d her against the fortifyed island & St. Johns. This day I wrote several letters to be ready to send by sum of the prisioners that are going home to New England. This after noon a whale boat was sent off with dispatches to Major Rogers, &c.

Saturday, 21 *June.* This day prou^d rainy. We spent the day in our tent writeing letters & disputeing sum points of concequence. At evening we drank to our wives & sweethearts, &c.

Sunday, 22^d *June.* This day prov^d very pleaseant. I was of duty. Should be glad to have some news from home to amuse my self. No regard is paid in general here to sacred time. This day I heard a band of musick at the commanding officers tent while they were dineing, which was very delightfull, tho in my opinion not so seasonable on such days of sacred appointment.

Monday, 23 *June.* This day was very rainy & wet. I kept in my tent most of the day. Toward night it cleard of. Sum of Major Rogers party arivd from a scout. At nine oclock in ye evening the Major came in himself, & 26 French prisioners with him, taken about 3 miles from St. John's Fort. He has destroy^d a small pequited fort & several houses, & a great quantity of provisions. This was effected without any blood shed or fireing a gun.

Tuseday, 24. This day fair & pleasant. I had the care of a 100 men to work in the King's Garden, which is the finest garden I ever saw in my life, having at least 10 acres inclosed, & mostly sow^d & improu^d. This day one of our pretenders to a commission was whipt — a 100 lashes at post for disobeying orders & insolent language.[1]

Wednsday, 25 *June.* This morning Capt Harris's company came up to ye incampment; brings no news or letters. This day, about 9 oclock A. M., a flag of truce arivd from Canada. There is a general officer in the flag of truce, & they was sent down directly to Gen! Amherst, who we hear set of 3 days agon from Shenaetada.[2] I hear, by Capt Harris, that Mr. Saml Berry is stationed at Fort Edward; is got so far promoted as to have a second lievtenancy with Capt Henry Brown.

Thirsday, 26 *June.* This day I took a quantity of stores of Mr. Forsey in order to supply my men. I rec^d a letter from Boston with Liev^t Richardsons commission in it. Went directly to the sutlers to wett it, so it might wear well withou cracking. Several battoes ariv^d here with provision from Ticondaroga. The weather clear & pleasant.

Fryday, 27 *June.* Today Col? Ingersoll & Major Willard & 4

---

[1] Sergeant Holden's Journal gives the name of John Bunker. 2 Proceedings, vol. iv. p. 393.

[2] Probably Schenectady.

cap.^{ts} & 300 men, were sent up the lake in order to cut timber to finish the works.[1] To day I am of duty; went to see the detachment imbarque. This day the prisioner that were sent hear by the enemy went off for New England & N. York.

Saturday, 28 *June*. To day I detacht 7 men of my company to go in the artelery under the command of Capt Jones. Went out to walk round to see the land; could see where the Indians used to carry our people in order to burn. I am told great numbers of them have been caried there to suffer to satisfie their insatiate loue of blood & cruelty. At night we followed the old custom of drinking to wives & swetthearts.

Sunday, 29 *June*. To day the weather is quite pleasant, — a rare thing in this part of the word. I see no regard paid to this day, without it is to put more men on duty. Can hear no news from home at all, no way.

Monday, 30 *June*, 1760. This day I have the pequit guard. Sent the Liev.^t & 36 men across the lake to git sum bark for the hospitall. The weather showrey. I wrote a letter home, having an oppertunity to send it directly to Boston. To day 2 men belonging to our troops was caryed to the hospital, being taken with the small pox.[2] I am in hopes it wont spread, for all possible care is taken to prevent it, the hospitall being 2 miles off the incampment; & our colonels have not had it; so they will, I trust, take the more care that it dont spread.

Tuseday, 1.st *July*, 1760. This day am off duty. This morning the brigg came up the lake from a cruize. She is a fine looking vessell, & it seem much as if I were at home, seeing a brig come in & come to anchor. We are mending the battoes, & every thing looks likely we shall move forward in about 20 days. To day my First Lev.^t & Serg.^t Martin & 3 privates my company went down the lake to relivee the regular troops stationd down there in the sloops. There went about 60 of the Provincials & Rhoad Island troops in the party. To day Ens.ⁿ Newhall of my company is on duty at drawing timber in to the fort. He has command of 80 men.

Wednsday, 2.^d *July*. To day I have the care of 280 men to work in the fort. To day Joseph Eaton of Capt Harts company died senseless, & in the evening one of Capt Jackson's men at roll calling answerd to his name, but before they had done he was dead. Col^o. Willard came to camp to day from New England. . . .

Thirsday, 3.^d *July*. To day I am off duty; went to view the works. There is a setler here has not obey^d the genr^l orders, but sold his liquors to the soldiers, & several of the regulars got drunk, & one of them broke open a markee & was whipt one thousand lashes. His liquors

---

[1] Col. Joseph Ingersoll and Major Caleb Willard. Holden's Journal makes a trifling difference in the numbers sent. See 2 Proceedings, vol. iv. p. 393.

[2] Ibid.

were seized & taken out of his store, to the number of one pipe of Bristoll beer & 3 quarter casks of wine, & stove to peices, & all the liquor lost; & another sutler for the like offence had 5 or 6 casks of liquors stove in like maner. So we have wine & strong beer running down our street.[1] In the evening we had very sharp thunder & lightning. The clouds run very low. I was never so sensible of the thunder being so nigh in my life. We have rain here almost every other day, otherwise there would nothing grow, for the ground is almost all clay, & in two days time if it be clear sunshine, it will bake so hard that no grass can grow.

Fryday, 4th *July*, 1760. To day I was ordred to hold a court martial at my tent, my self president, for the tryall of Peter Jones a private in Cap! Martin's company, confin[d] by Cap! Abial Peirce for denying his duty & insolent language. The members, being 4 liev[ts], were assembled. The prisioner was brought, & the crime read. He pleaded ignorance of the facts aledged against him, as also his being in liquor & knew not what he did. Cap! Peirce was then cal[d], who prou[d] the fact by Cap! Hart, who was present & heard him deny & abuse Cap! Peirce. The prisoner's own officer then came & said that the said Jones was very apt to be depriv[d] of his reason by the smallest quantity of spiritous liquor. The prisoner was then sent back to the guard house. The court after having debated and considred on the nature of the crime & the mans constitution, they resolv[d] he should receive 50 stripes on his naked back with a cat nine tails. The result being carry[d] to the commanding officer, he approu[d] of it as just & right. There was myself & 2 other of the court had never been on court martials; we went & was shod according to custom. This evening at releiving the pequit the s[d] Jones rec[d] his punishment. To day Brigadier General Ruggles ariv[d] here from New England.

Saturday, 5th *July*. This day was very sultry, hot. I took a walk round the incampment. There came in 6 Oneida Indians,[2] & brought in one scalp. There is a rumer in camp that there is 300 Canada Indians a comeing to joyn us, being discouraged with the bad luck the Monsiuers have. I hear like wise that our General Murry at Quebeck hangs all without distinction who were in the capitulation last year at the surender of Quebeck, & that have assisted the French at the late attempt on that fortress. To day I heard that Col° Montgomery has had a skirmish with the Cherokee Indians, & kill[d] 100 of them, & burnt 3 towns. At night we concluded by drinking to wives and sweet hearts, which is as duly obseru[d] here as any of our duty. There is one more

---

[1] See Sergeant Holden's Journal of the same date. One of the sutlers was named George Morris. 2 Proceedings, vol. iv. p. 394.

[2] These Indians are mentioned by Sergeant Holden, Ibid.

of Capt Harts men dead to day. Through God's goodness, I hant lost one man of my company yet, nor is any of them sick ; it is a general time of health in camp. Can hear no news from home. Yesterday was in company with the Gentlemen Commissioners from old York, who are well acquainted with my relations there, who were all well when they set off.

Sunday, 6 July. To-day it is extreame hot. I took a walk about 2 miles in the wood to see the carpenters; returned & wrote 2 letters to send home. We have no appearance of any divine worship in our camp, & I can see no defirence in regard to the day. I spent most of the day in my tent writeing & reading. Ens^n Newhall is on duty drawing timber. I hear 2 of our New England men are dead of the small pox at the hospitall, & I hear that the French will give up Montreal without fighting any more. The news about Col' Montgomery is confirm^d.

Monday, 7th July. Took a walk down to the landing. Return^d to breackfast, & rec^d a letter from my brother Jenks, dated 9 June, 1760, with the agreable news of their being all in health at that time. To day I begun to build me a booth, but before it was finished I had orders to move to the right of the incampment, being in the first battallion of Brigadier Genrael Ruggles's reg^t, & so must move my booth or loose all my leabour. There is eleven companys in the first battallion, & 10 in the second. Colonell Richard Saltonstall comands the first battallion under the Brigadier.

Tuseday, 8 July, 1760. This morning we were alarm^d about 6 oclock by the enemy, who fell upon a party of Major Rogers' rangers, just by their incampment on the other side the lake, all in sight of our incampment, & they have kill^d one on the spot & wounded six more, who are brought over to the hospitall. I have been down to see them, & 4 of them are mortally woundid, — 2 shot through their bodys, & 1 shot through his head, the other through both thighs; the 2 others may, with good care, git well. It was a very affecting sight to see the poor creatures lay weltering in their blood & fainting with death in their countenance.[1] Immediately Major Rogers with his rangers ran out of their breast work & pursued the enemy, who are almost all French, but very few Indians among the party. Tis suppos^d there was 300 in their party, & the regular light infantry & severall large partys of regulars to intercept them ; & a sub of our troops & 25 men was sent down to the sloops to give them inteligence. It was a bold action, right in plain view of our forts & camps, & but a little way from Major Rogers incampment, & on the same side the lake; we have seen part of the rangers return, but what news I cannot learn. The same day we were setled & regimented, & I am in Col° Salton-

[1] Cf. Holden's Journal of the same date, 2 Proceedings, vol. iv. p. 894.

stons battalion, which is the first in the regiment, commanded by Brigadier General Ruggles. We then struck our tents & incampt on the right of all the Massachusetts troops. Both the brigadiers battallions, — Col° Tho' regiment on the left & Col° Willard in the center. Those captains belonging to the first battallion, after our being rankᵈ, all went to the sutlers & drank to our better acquaintance, & then returnd, mutually satisfyed with our lots; & I am exceediugly rejoycᵈ that it was my lot to fall amongst such agreable officers.

Wednsday, 9 July. This day am off duty, & have built us a fiue booth. At the door of my tent, the weather extreame hot. Took a walk after dinner. Can hear no news in camp, only disputeing of rank amongst officers, & whiping sutlers & soldiers. At evening had a letter from Lᵗ Richardson, who is well, but not content with his station. Major Rogers is returnᵈ without overtakeing the enemy; the wounded men are all alive yet, but I dont think they can live long.

Thirsday, 10th July. This day is very sultry, hot. I am off duty, building me another booth. Ensⁿ Newhall is on a court martial. I let the president hold his court at my tent, because his had no booth finishᵈ for his conveniency. I find this climate vastly hotter than I ever expected. I think it has been much hotter this 6 or 7 days than I ever kuew so many together in New England. Two of the wounded men of the rangers is dead; & Jacob Hallowell, that was wounded in Rogers' fight before, is also dead of his wounds.

Fryday, 11 July, 1760. Continues very hot & dry. I am on duty, & Ensⁿ Newhall with me; we were drawing timber out in the wood; have 100 men; & we all cary our arms out since the enemy fell on Rogers's working party. To day I recᵈ a letter from my own partner, the only one I have recᵈ from her since I left home, dated 8 June, & one from Brother Nathan, dated 9 June, with the most agreable news of their being in health. Lᵗ Pope came up from Ticondaroga, & brought these letters & a number of others from New England. Expect soon to move forward.

Saturday, 12 July, 1760. Continues extreame hot & dry. To day I found that James Casey & Wm Delarue had got orders on the sutler & forged my name to them & taken a considerable up. I immediately sent them under guard, & acquainted Col° Saltonstal of their crime, who advised me not to send their crime in as forgery, because then they must come to a general court martial & be tryᵈ for their lives, & it is death by the martial law for a soldier to counterfit his officers hand; but told me to send in their crime as ill behaviour & insolent treatment, which I accordingly did, & by that means hope their lives will be saved by trying them by a regimental court martial. To day Mr. Furnance, our brigade major, arivᵈ from New England. I sent 2 letters

for home by Serg⁺ Fullinton, of Cap⁺ Harris's company, who has orders
to go to Albany. At night we drank to wives & sweethearts, & so
concluded the day. More news of going forward.

Sunday, 13 July. This morning I went to the sutlers & searched all
my orders, & found that Henry Bony & Jacob Hasey had orders on
him that was counterfit. I immediately sent the gent⁺ under guard, &
the Brigadier ordred a court martiall on them; but I got him to put it
off untill to morrow. To day L⁺ Richmond confind a regular to our
guard for abusive language, & just as our pequit was releivd & gone to
their tent, there came about 40 of the granadiers with clubs & forced
our quarter guard & took away the prisoner. The guard pursued as
fast as possible, & pequit was turnd out, & all pursud, & recovered 2
of the mob; they fird 2 guns at the granadiers; I beleive wounded
sum. This affair put the whole of the line in commotion; all the regular regiments were turnd out in an instant & drawn up in order, supposeing it was an enemy; how ever, we were soon in quiet. 2 of the
offenders was securd, & will no doubt meet with a punishment ade-
quate to their crimes. I can see no distintion paid to the day except
the flags flying & more men put on duty, & almost always sum develish
pranck playd, &c.

Monday, July 14ᵗʰ. This day, about 7 o'clock A. M., there was a
regimental court martial held at the presidents tent, who was Cap⁺
Chadbourn; after the prisoners was brought & exam⁺, Casey & Delaru
confesed they were guilty of the facts, but the other 2 pleaded not
guilty; but Hasey own⁺ he saw Delarue sign his order, but it appeard
Bony knew nothing of his signing his. The court sentenced Casey 250
stripes, Delarue 150, & Hasey 50; which the Brigadier approu⁺ off as
just. At releiving the quarter guard, these fellows was brought forth &
rec⁺ their punishment.[1] I ordred the serjants to turn out all my company to see them go through the opperation, to deter any from such vile
practises. I had rather lost 20 dollers than such affairs should a hapned in my company. Ens⁺ Newhall has been on com⁺ up to Ticondaroga today. L⁺ Richardson sent of for stores which I sent him.
Heard a rumor of Esq Goldthwaits comeing up pay master of our
troops; I fear too good news to be true.

Tuseday, July 15. The weather continues extreame hot & dry. I
have the care of a 100 men for to make fachines & gabions & erecting
a fachine batery in ord⁺ to practise the men as Lord Louden did at
Halifax. I had an easy tour, for I went out at 5 o'clock in the morning & return⁺ @ 8, & then went out again at 5 in the afternoon &
return in at gun firing. We have continual whiping of sum or other in

---

[1] The record of this and the preceding two days amplifies the account of
Sergeant Holden, under date of July 14, 2 Proceedings, vol. iv. p. 394.

the line. To day Col° Saltonston told me my friend Esqr Goldthwait was certainly coming up to pay of our troops.

Wednesday, 16 *July*. To day am of duty. Got sundry of stores of Mr. Hobbey for my company. We had news in camp that there was 12,000 French comeing up the lake, & that they had taken our 3 sloops that are cruizeing down the lake, — camp news, I beleive. To day I read a New York paper of the 30 June, & find the news exactly true that ye prisones brought in here the 19th of June conserning the raising the seige of Quebeck. In the after noon went to se the train practise in throwing shells. They hove 12 in all; it was a pleasant sight to see them flying in the air. Our people has caught two fawns alive in the lake, & there is plenty of them in these parts.

Thirsday, 17th *July*. To day am off duty. The weather continues hot & dry. I spent most part of the day in my tent a overhawling orders & settling accounts, & seeing that my companys tents well barked over the bottom, according to Brigadier General Ruggles order. In the afternoon walkd round the camp to pass away time & to divert our selves. Hear that Genl Amherst set off from Oneida Lake the 9 instant for Oswago, & expect to move forward in about 12 days from here. To day Ensn Newhall is on pequit.

Fryday, 18th *July*, 1760. Very hot & no signs of rain, which is very much wanted here, for if it continues such weather a few days longer, all the fine gardens we have here will be intirely dryd up, & all the fruits perish. This morning Capt Hart & I went to view the fachine battery, which is a most finished & looks very beautifull. Returnd & have been calculating how far we are from home, & find it by the best judges 190 miles to Boston by No. 4. So then I am nearer home than when I was at Albany, altho I have traveled a 100 miles from Albany. To day the train are practiseing their mortars in throwing shells, & our troops have drawn 6 rounds pr man in order to fire at a mark. In the afternoon we had a fine refreshing shower. Cleard up & quite cool & pleasant. There was two of the regular officers fought a duel with pistols. They made 2 tryalls, but did not wound neither. This evening we was drawn up on the parade & had prayers performd by a chaplain[1] from New England. He is the only one of that cloath that has joynd us yet.

Saturday, 19th *July*, 1760. This morning went to see the train practise throwing of shells. They made several very good shotts. Returnd & went to view the fachine battery. This day about 500 troops went across the lake to git spruse; nothing meterial hapned. This day there is a post arived from Oswago. At night we concluded by drinking to wives & sweethearts, which is as constantly observd as any duty we have in camp. Pleasant weather to day.

[1] See Sergeant Holden's Journal, 2 Proceedings, vol. iv. p. 395.

Sunday, 20 *July*. To day am off duty. It has been my luck as yet not to be on any duty of a Sunday. To day I wrote a letter to send home, & spent most of the day in my tent writeing & reading. The weather very hot; much hotter than is used to be in New England. At night we had prayers in the camp. No news from home, which is the scarcest of any thing in camp; for we have ladys enough in town, & they are walking out with the regular officers to take y° evening air every night.

Monday, 21ˢᵗ *July*. To day I have the care of a party of men to work in the fort drawing the timber up on the walls. Was very agreably entertaind on the works by the company of a regular officer who lately came from captivaty in Montreal, & reading the Spectator. Towards night the brigg[1] came down from Ticondaroga, haveing been up to clean & grave. The weathr prety pleasant. I have a bad boil on my right wrist, which is very troublesome.

Tuseday, 22ᵈ *July*. The large English sloop has come down last night, & all things preparing to proceed down the lake. Went this morning with Capᵗ Hart & Ensⁿ Newhall down to the wharfe to see the shiping & the preparations going on. In returning to camp Ensⁿ Newhall is taken very ill with a vomiting. I immediately by his desire got the docter to come to him, & he has gave him sumthing which I hope by Gods blessing will cary off his illness. Went after diner to view the fachine battery. Rogers's men are practiseing at shooting at marks. We have very hot dry weather, the days much hotter than in New England, but the nights are as cold as we have in September, for I can not lay warm in my blanket towards day, but in the day can hardly bear any cloaths on. By the best information I can git we shall move forward in first week in August. We are preparing all things necessary to forward the opperations. This evening Ensⁿ Newhall is much better.

Wednsday, 23ᵈ *July*, 1760.[2] This morning there is a general court martial, held at Brigadier General Ruggles tent, himself presedent, for the tryall of all prisoners that are brought before them. Lᵗ Richmond of Colᵒ Thomas's regᵗ is brought on tryall, confind by the comᵈ officer Colᵒ Havertin for disobedience of orders. This morning Ensⁿ Newhall is got prety comfortable again; he has had a very sharp turn, but hope is out of danger of being sick. In the afternoon had a letter from Leutenant Richardson from on board one of the sloops that are down the lake, with news of their being all well that belong to me. I prepared a quantity of stores to send them down, but am informᵈ they are ordred up; so I deferᵈ sending them. The brigg has been firing 2 rounds to clear her guns. The train & rangers & all the troops except the provincials are practiseing.

[1] See Sergeant Holden's Journal, 2 Proccedings, vol. iv. p. 395.
[2] See page 40.

Thirsday, 24ᵗʰ *July*, 1760. To day am off duty. Went to see where they have been throwing bombs. They have measurd out a 1000 yards, & set stakes at every 50 yards with the number on them. Here is one of my men that was stationed at Ticondaroga, come up with a setler who has brought up a very fine mistress with him. On their passage they fell into disputes. At length he struck her, which inraged hir so that after several fits & efforts jumpt over board. This coolᵈ her courage, for her sweetheart held her under water untill she was amost expiring. They then took her in, stript off her cloaths & drest anew, & so the fray ended. I wish it were the fate of all these sort of ladys that follow the army. She apeard prety likely & was very well drest. This day proues rainy, which is very much wanted in this dark corner of the earth. At night 2 of our sloops came up from a cruize. I hear Lᵗ Richardson is on board one of them.

Fryday, *July* 25ᵗʰ, 1760. Went this morning on board the sloop where Lievᵗ Richardson & part of my company is. Found them all in good health. Brought the lievtenant on shore. The news in camp is that Genˡ Amherst, attempting to go down a falls, was attact by the enemy & lost 1000 men & is now comeing back to go this way. I likwise heard the French had blown up the fortifyd island & goue, & that Genˡ Murry had laid seige to Montreal, & that it is a establisht peace at home, &c.

Saturday, *July* 26ᵗʰ, 1760. This day off duty; the weather rainy. I kept cheifly in my tent. Ensⁿ Newhall remains ill. Lᵗ Richardson on shore, wee all practiseing drinking to wives & sweethearts, & I am warnd this evening to go on command to Ticondaroga to morrow for provisions. A regular captain commands the whole detachment. Nothing occourd to day remarkable.

Sunday, 27ᵗʰ *July*, 1760. This morning was on the parade at revaloes beating for go with the detachment to the mill for provision. It raind prety much, but the wind is fair. We set off about 7 oclock A. M.; had a fine gale all the way, but much rain. Got there about noon. There was about 500 in the party. We could not git boats enough for the whole, so came back 10 in battoe. We rendavousd at Ticondaroga fort. I went to view the fortifications. They are advantageously built & very strong & pleasantly scituated. We all set of again about 5 oclock P. M. The weather is clearᵈ up quite pleasant & calm. We all made the best of our way for our station. I arivd about nine oclock at night at my tent. This is the first Sunday I have been on duty up here. There was divine service performd in camp to day. But I have not had the luck of hearing one sermon since I left home. I hear to day that the recruits raised in our provinc are on their march. Query, will they arive before December.

Monday, 28ᵗʰ *July*. This morning went down to the landing for to see the boats vnloaded. The weather is fair, serene, cool, & pleasant, with a fine breeze to the westward. I spent most of the day in walking round the fort landing & places ajacant. The fleet is fiting out with all expedition & makes a very fine appearance. I hope we shall soon pay Monsiuers a vissit at the Ile aux Noix. No extraordinaries hapned to day.

Tuseday, 29th *July*, 1760. To day am off duty. L! Richardson has saild again down the lake on a cruize to releive the other sloop. To day there was a large pekerell found on the shore. It measurd 4 feet 5 inches in length & waid, as is reported, 35 lb. Towards night the sloop that was stationed down the lake came up. Most part of this day I spent in walking round the camp & forts. There is a party sent to carry provisions to the Hamshire troops.

Wednsday, 30th *July*. To day am off duty. Spent most of the day in the tent in writeing and posting of my accounts. This after noon a droue of cattle came from No. 4. At the evening wrote a letter to send home by the drovers. Ens? Newhall is got quite well again. No news from home, altho there comes plenty of letters in camp, yet none for me.

Thirsday, 31st *July*. To day wrote letters & made up 2 packquets for my men to send home to New England. Have spent part of the day with Cap! Hart in his tent & several other gentlemen disputeing on the carrage & deferent disposition of the fair sex. This afternoon the Hamshire troops are ariv⁴. They were obliged to quit the road & come forward because the could not git a supply of provisions that way.

Fryday, 1st *of August*, 1760. This morning I awoke & found my tent all flood with water, — about 4 inches over the floor. I got a number of my men to dig a trench to drean of the water. To day have y° care of a party of men to take the number of battoes that are assin⁴ to our battallion. We rec⁴ 80 battoes for all the Massachusetts troops, & brought them to a convenient place & sunk them for to keep them tight, & set a guard over them.

Saturday, 2d *August*. To day am off duty. There is about 120 seamen draughted out to go on board the brig [1] & sloops; they are this day sail⁴ on a cruize down the lake. Its said they are to take post at an island 7 miles a this side Ile aux Noix, & a rumor prevails that we shall send a 1,000 men down there to incamp till the whole arives. A evening we followed the delightful custom of remembering wives & sweathearts.

Sunday, 3d *Aug*, 1760. I find tis the Lords Day by the flags flying, as its the only visible sign of the day amongst us. Went to view the Hamshire incampment & the mark that is made to fire cannon shott at. The weather very hot to day. Cap! Aaron Willard ariv⁴ from

[1] The name of the brig was "Duke Cumberland." See Sergeant Holden's Journal, 2 Proceedings, vol. iv. p. 395.

No. 4. I hear the recruits are on their way up here a this side Albany. To day divine service was perform^d at our perrade by one of our chaplains.

Monday, 4th *Aug^t*, 1760. This morning lowery & rainy. I am of duty to day; spent my time in tent writeing & reading & posting of accounts. I have 12 of my men detacht this morning to go over the lake to cut timber. In the after noon it cleard up quite pleasant. As I walk^d out to amuse my self down to the landing & round the incampment, I heard of the approach of the recruits; hope to have news from home by them. I expect them here this week.

Tuseday, 5th *August*. I understand that Mr. Farrington has agreed to ride as post to New England, to carry letters at six pence, Yorke currency, a peice; he purposses to make 2 trips this campeign. I wrote several letters to send by him. I went over the lake to see Rogers's incampment which is very pleasant. There is a fine hospatall rais^d to day for our troops. The afternoon spent in walking out, & riteing in my tent. Have nothing extraordinary to day.

Wednsday, 6 *Aug^t*, 1760. To day am off duty; went to see the artelery practise at fireing shott. To day, about noon Esqr Goldthwait ariv^d from New England; he is, as I understand, pay master gen^l of our troops. He brought me the most agreable news I have heard in camp; that is, I mean the news of my wife & freind being in health. I rec^d 3 letters, — one from her, one from brother Jenks, & one from brother Nathan Sergant.

Thirsday, 7th.[1] To day am off duty; spent most of the day in camp. I hear the recriuts are all on their way up here; sum of the officers are arived all ready. We have orders to be ready to imbarque a Sunday next for St. Johns. I hope to be able in short time to give a good account of sum part of Canada if its the will of God, & my Col° orders me to move on with the troops. No extraordinaries to day. Shiping shott & shells.

Fryday, 8th *Aug^t*. To day wrote a letter, & sent it in Mrs. Goldthwaits by Mr. Farrington, who set of to day for Boston, & is to return immediately after his business is done. Mr. Goldthwait intends to begin paying the soldiers tomorrow morning. This evening all the detachments are comeing in, except those all ready gone forward, in order to prepare them selves for to imbarque.

Saturday, 9th *August*, 1760. This morning all my men rec^d one dollar a peice that desir^d it, to git them sum necessarys to carry with them down the lake. I have been packing up mine & giting sum stores for me on the lake, if I am ordred. It is not known who goes or stays as yet. At night we drank to wives & sweethearts. I hear Lt Col° Hawkes is to tarry behind.

---

[1] See page 46.

Sunday, Aug. 10th, 1760. Orders to be ready to imbarque tomorrow morning. I spent most of the day in packing up my things. I left my coat & jackett & all my writeings with Esq. Goldthwait & one johannas in cash, to be kept till I return ; or if I am not to return,.to be sent home. I lost 2 of my best shirts to day by a washer woman.

Monday, 11th *August.* This morning at 10 oclock A.M., we struck our tents & marcht down to the battoes, in order to imbarque for S. Johns. The Brigadier led the whole of the Massachusetts troops. At noon we sett of in three colums ; the wind blood prety fresh a head. We rowd till about sunsett when the signall was made to form to the left, or west, shore, & then we landed and the pequit made the guard. We have come about 6 miles.

Tuseday, 12 *Aug.* The morning very calm, only a small breeze to ye southward. We set off in order about sunrise ; I had very hard lodging on the barrells in the battoe last night. After roweing about 3 or 4 miles, the wind came right ahead, so that the Ligoneir was obliged to anchor the rest of the fleet. Kept along until the wind blood prety fresh ; orders came to cross the lake to the east side, where we all came to land in a bay called Button Mold Bay, where we are to tarry all night. Here Cap. Shores [1] got his dismission from his Majesties service to return to New England.

Wednesday, Aug. 13th, 1760. We tarry'd in the morning a while for the Ligoneir to come up ; set of about 8 oclock A.M. Haveing come about 18 miles from Crown Point, we passed through the Narrows, which is very mountainous on the west side, but very plain, flat land on the east. We proceeded forward till about noon, when the wind sprung up quite fresh ahead ; we kept on untill about 4 oclock P.M., when we landed on the west side the lake. We are now about 28 miles from Crown Point. Here we have news from the brigg & sloops ; they have had a brush with the Monseiurs, & droue them back to the island. I lodged much better last night than y' night before.

Thursday, 14th *Aug.* This morning the wind came fare & the Ligoneir came up. We put of about sunrise, & stood along down the lake with all sail spread, & made a fine appearance. We kept on till about 11 oclock A.M., when the wind blood quite hard, & raind very much. We were obliged every one to shift for themselves ; a prodigeous sea & hard wind obliged us to make a harbour on y' north side of an island called Scuylers Island. We have lost 7 rangers [2] by the cannoe spliting, & 2 of the recruits fell over & was drownd ; one kill'd by accident, & there is several battoes missing, I fear in bad circumstances. We came to day about 45 miles.

---

[1] See Sergeant Holden's Journal under date of August 13, 2 Proceedings, vol. iv. p. 397.

[2] Ibid.

Fryday, 15ᵗʰ *Aug*. This morning is lowrey, & the wind prety fresh, but fair; we set off about sunrise and made all sail, as much as we could suffer, a prodigeous sea going. The land is all flat & level, hardly any hills or mountains to be seen, & what is at a great distance. Expect to be amongst bad neighbours before night. God grant we may behave ourselves like men, & play the man for the city & people of our God, & let him do as seamest him best. I lodged these two nights past very comfortablely in my battoe; most of the troop lodged on shore by large fires.

Saturday, 16ᵗʰ *Aug*. We set of from an island called Ile a mot;[1] it is about 18 miles to the fortifyd island from here. I lodg in the battoe very comfortable. It was about the dawning of the day when we put of; after rowing across a large bay we form⁴ the line, 2 boats abrest. I beleive the whole reachd 4 miles, & made a very beautifull appearance. The weather quite pleasant with a small breze in our feavour. Thus Providence seems to smile on our proceedings. After entering the Narrows, which is not more than a musket shott across, & very intricate, the enemy's schooner & reddow came out to meet us, but was droue back. We formed for landing in about a mile & $\frac{1}{2}$ from the enemy's fort, with all our battoes a brest, to land on the east shore. As soon as the signall for landing was made, we all rowd right to shore, & landed in extreme good order without any molestation at all. The Ligoneir redows[2] & prows kept a fire on the enemys fort & vessells, to feavour our landing; after which we marcht up & formd a line, & set out our pequits. The land we marcht through exceeding wett & mirey. I went sum times almost up to my middle in mud & water, & obliged to run most of the way to keep up with the front. We then set about makeing a breast work which was compleated in a little time, as the men are in high spirits. The vessell keeps fireing on the French; but Monsiuers are not so complesant as to answer them, which we impute to their want of men or ammunition. We haveing a little rum, we made sum toddy to keep up the custom of Saturday night health.

Sunday, 17ᵗʰ *Aug*. I lodged last night on the ground without my blanket, only a few bushes to cover me, & as wett as could well be, but through Divine goodness rested very well. No enemy to molest us in our breastwork, which was kept well man⁴ all night. One of our redows going to reconitre the forts was fired on by the enemy, & Capt. Ghaye[8] of the Royall Artelery was killd, & 5 or six more lost their legs. One of these unfortunate men belongs to my company, & has his leg cut off; I hear he is like to recover. The rest of the day spent in fixing a shed to lodg under. I have not had my cloaths of since I left Crown

---

[1] Ile a mot is Ile au Noix. See Sergeant Holden's Journal, 2 Proceedings, vol. iv. p. 397.

[2] Probably radeau, mentioned Ibid.

[8] Clagg, according to Sergeant Holden's Journal, Ibid.

Point; am obliged to lay with my arms and ammunition all on, to be ready in case of need.

Monday, 18th *Aug*!, 1760.   Last night I had the pequit, & kept one quarter of it standing centry at a time all night.   I had 2 subs who took care of the pequit, & I lay in my bower till break of day, & slept comfortablely ; in the morning was ordred out to cover a party of fasshine makers in the woods, about ½ mile from the breast work.   The enemy have fired several cannon to day at our people, but done no execution. We have taken possission of a point of land right opposite the island, & within muskett shott of the fort where we are erecting batterys.   At night was releivd by Capt! Barnard.

Tuseday, 19th *Aug*!   Last night I had my tent set up, & lay like a minister all night; this morning we had orders to pack up every thing for to moue on to the Point to cover the batterys.   Marcht off about 11 oclock A. M., through extream bad way, to the Point, & built a fine breastwork in front, & begun one in the rear.   The enemy heard us incamping, & they kept firing cannon at us, but hurt none of the men, tho our camp is not half cannon shot from the enemys fort, & nothing to hinder but only the trees, & them not very thick.

Wednsday, 20th *Aug*!, 1760.   Last night raind sum.   I lay in my tent all night without any molestation.   The enemy have not fired a gun all night.   This morning there came one of the enemy to our people, & what storey he tells I can not learn, I hear it so many defirent ways; but by all I think the enemy very scant of men on the island.   In the afternoon they fired very briskly on our men, but did no great dammage,— ōly wounded one man with a grape shot slightly.   We go on briskly with our batterys, & hope in a few days to give Monsiuers a salute ; for they begin to grow very quarelsome of late, & wont let us live in peace by y^m.[1]

Thirsday, 21st *Aug*!   Last night it rained pretty much.   However, it did not hinder our people from working on the battery.   To day I am ordred to assist the engineer ; I have a party of 150 men, 2 subs, 4 serg^ts in carrying timber to the batterys ; there is 800 of the provincials of us on fatigue in building batterys to day, under the care of Col° Saltonstall.   The enemy kept a constant fire on us most part of the day, firing 12, 9, & six pound shot & langrege ; they wounded 10 men, 5 of which, I beleive, mortally, the other not bad.   I escaped my self very narrowly several times.   I think it very remarkable that the enemy have not killd great numbers, when we are so much exposed.   Our redows have fired several shott on them to day.

Fryday, 22d.   Last night just as I had got to bed, being much fatigued, the whole army was ordred to arms immidiately, haveing dis-

---

[1] Compare the entries for 19th and 20th August with those of Sergeant Holden's Journal for the same date. 2 Proceedings, vol. iv. p. 398.

coverd a large party of the enemy set off from the island in battoes & putting over towards us. After we had put out all fires in camp & man^d the breast work, there came orders to return to our tents, except the pequit; for the enemy, finding they were discovered, ruturn back without fireing a gun. However, we lay in readiness to receive them if they should attempt it again ; & about an hour before day, a regular centry, supposeing he heard sum of them, fired his peice, as did 3 or 4 more, which alarmd us again, & all turnd out and man^d the breast work, waiting for them. In a few minutes, the cap^t of the pequit, thinking he saw a man without the lines, challenged it 3 times, & nothing answering, fired his peice : & sum body at the same time gave the word to fire, when the whole of our battallion mostly discharged their peices, which spread almost the line, it being impossible to stop our men from fireing, altho there was no enemy near us. We soon found our mistake, & returnd to our tents. We have got a fine breast work, both in front & rear, & have cut all the trees & cleard them out of our camp to prevent our being hurt by the limbs falling that are shot of by ye enemys cannon. This morning we are clearing a road through our camp to draw cannon across below the enemys fort, to erect a battery on a point of land in order to cut off all communication between them & St. Johns. We have landed all our morters & got them up to the bomb-battery, & are gitting the cannon on shore & drawing them to the batterys, & hope to have three batterys opened by night. I hear a scout of our rangers have taken 4 prisoners this morning. Nothing meteral has hapned to day ; the enemy have been prety quiet, & hant fired abowe 5 or six cannon to day & a few small armes, & done no damage, as I can hear. There was a man of Capt Harriss taken up for dead, — hurt by a tree falling on him.

Saturday, 23^d *Aug^t*, 1760. Last night we had no molestation from the enemy. Our batterys are almost compleat, & the brig has sent on shore to git fasshines to hang over on her sides, so as to atteck the fort at the same time the batterys are opened. The enemy have kill^d & scalp^t one of our men last night where we first landed ; a party of our rangers fired across to the island last night & kill^d 4 of the French. I hear the batterys opening will be preceeded first by all the drums beating a point of war, next by a band of musick, followd by all the provincials singing psalmes. About 3 oclock P. M., all our batterys was opened & gave the French a fine salute, which Monsiuers did not return ; the artelery kept playing constantly, & did great execution. A little while after, one of our soldiers fired his peice ; Col^o Saltonstall immediatly ordred a court martial on him, which fell to be my tour of duty. I, immediately after the members was assembled, held it at my tent. I ordred the prisoner to be brought, who pleaded ignorance of the guns being charg^d ; on ye whole the court sentenced him 40 stripes, which was approud of by Col⁰ Saltonstall. But when he was stript & brought to yᵉ post, the Col⁰ was so good as to forgive his punishment.

Sunday, 24ᵗʰ *Augt.* This morning I wrote a letter & sent it to Crowwn Point to Esqʳ Goldthwait, to acquaint him I was well, & desireing him to write that I was so in his letter. I had no sleep last night, for our people was cuting away the boom, & the enemy would fire volleys of small arms on them, & then our battery would return it with grape shott, & the morters was kept going all night, which made it seem that the elements was all fire & smoak. Our people has almost efected cutting away the boom. The French has not fired a cannon since our batterys was opened this morning. 9 of the French battoes was seen going off towards St. Johns, & 2 more went last night, so I believe the enemy will all leave yᵉ island shortly.

Monday, 25ᵗʰ *Augᵗ,* 1760. Last night I had the pequit. In the evening Ensn. Warren of Capᵗ Jones company was shot in his back by a muskett ball; the ball lodgᵈ in his body. A serj of yᵉ Massachusetts had both his hands shot away at the same time, & several more wounded. One of my company has recᵈ a ball in his arm; the ball was cut out, the bone is not hurt. I kept up all night walking round our battallion to keep the centry right; for if any disorder happens, the blame would lay on me. The night quite pleasant & bright moon shine; the battery would fire a round about once an hour & throw shells about as often. In the morning I sent a serjᵗ & 8 men to carry Ensⁿ Warren to yᵉ hospitall, who I dont think will live 24 hours longer; he has been a very good officer & bhaved well. About 9 oclock we heard a great number of small arms fireing down along the lake side, & sum cannon. Immediately all the pequits was turnd out to assist Major Rogers, who it seems had engaged the French vessels. We all marcht out, our Provincial pequits servᵈ as front, rear, & flank guards to the regulars. I went with my pequit in the advance guard. Just as we had joynd the party already out, the fire ceased; & we halted and set out centry, for we suspected the enemy had a large party on the land sumwhere near us. In a few minutes a regular officer brought us the joyfull news that the French great redow,¹ thir brigg, & sloop had struck to us; we then marcht down to the point of land where the cannon was, & saw the vessells al laying there under English coulours. We have not lost a man in this affair, altho the action was very sharp & no batery for the cannon to play behind. Monsuirs has no vessell now on the lake except a row galley & battoes. We have killd a feild officer of theirs who was on board, & have taken their commodore & about 20

¹ Sergeant Holden's Journal says, "one rideau, one topsail schooner, and a sloop.'

men prisoners. These prisoners inform us that we kill⁰ 180 of their men that day. We opened our batterys beside the wounded. They are very short of provision & ammunition, & can git no releif, now we have got their fleet; for we cut of all communication between them & S! Johns. In our marching into camp we met our comodore & a large party of sailors going down to man our new fleet. In the evening sum whale boats was carryed across to cut off the enemys retreat; & this night sum of the brigs cannon was carry across to put into the French vessells.

Tusday, 26ᵗʰ *August*, 1760.[1] This morning we have news by an express from Gen¹ Murrey, who writes that he has been joyned by 2 regiments from England & by the garisson of Louisbourg, & that he intends the first fair wind to sail & invest Montreal, & desires us not to think hard if he reaps the glory of takeing Montreal, & that he has provisions enough for all three of the armys. We likewise hear that Gen! Amherst was 3 days agon within 30 miles of Montreal, & we have heard cannon fired several times at a distance that way. Gen¹ Murry was incampt at a place cal⁴ Sir Ells,[2] & the express was 9 days a comeing here; so by all curcumstances I beleive Montreal actually invested by Gen¹ Murrey. We are makeing up a party of the best men for the woods to go with Major Rogers; where they are destin⁴ I cannot yet tell. This afternoon a party of the provincials was ordrd on board the French prizes; Cap⁴ Hart went out of our battallion & 3 of my men. Just at night we opened a new battery down by the lower end of the island.

Wednsday, 27ᵗʰ.[1] Last night nothing worth notice hapned. This morning we had smart firing on both sides. The enemy have playd their cannon brisker to day than they have done any time before, but done no execution of any valve. A soldier of mine going with a dollar in his hand to the sutlers & a nine pound shot strake his hand, which only grazed the skin, but lost his dollar, & one of yᵉ Hamshire men wounded, which is all they have done, as I hear. About 3 oclock P. M. we was alarm⁴ by a sudden explosion.[3] At first we thought that the enemy had opened a larg battery, but we was soon inform⁴ that a number of our shells & sum powder at the 12 gun battery took fire by sum accident unknown; about 30 shells burst by this means, & 3 men kill⁴ out right & several others wounded. The enemy have kept a very smart fire all day, but done us no damage worth notice. All this we take as their last words.

Thirsday, 28ᵗʰ *August*, 1760, M⁴ This morning we found that the enemy had deserted & left yᵉ island. Immediately the granadiers & light infantry went over & took possession of that fortress. I hear

---

[1] See page 46. [2] Perhaps Sorel.
[3] See Sergeant Holden's Journal of the same date, 2 Proceedings, vol. iv. p. 399.

that the French commander has left orders that no provincial, ranger, or Indian be allow⁴ to go on the island; which orders I think is going to be follow⁴, for several of our officers endeavouring to go across, haveing got liberty of the Brigadier, were prevented by the regulars, which is look⁴ upon a very high affair, when we have done most part of the fatigue dureing the seige, & our men have been more exposed than they, must now be denyd the liberty to go & se what they have fought for. This day I have the care of a 100 men in order to draw the cannon out of our batterys down to wharfe & git them on board the vessells, in order to follow the enemy, who ran away to Saint Johns; we have got all of them down except one hoit & all the shott & shells & platforms; & this day our brigg & sloop passed by the island, haveing cut away the French boom that lay across. I hope soon to be able to give an account of Saint Johns. There is sum gent! officers that are very breif about to day to see the batterys & island that was poorly all the while the siege lasted.

Friday, 29th *August.* This morning lay in my tent till eight oclock, being very much fatigued last night with my days work. I hapned to hear of a gent! going to New England. I immediately wrote a letter to my partner at home, & sent it in one inclosed to Esqʳ Goldthwait, who told me that if I sent so he would inclose it in his & so send it home, which is the surest way I have to send. In the afternoon had all my things pact up in order to imbarque for St Johns. I hear Genˡ Amherst is got nigh to Montreal, & we shall soon be there, if the enemy dont hinder us.

Saturday, 30th *Aug*ᵗ, 1760. This morning about day break I got up to git my baggage on board in order to imbarque for Sᵗ Johns, & struck our tents ½ an hour after revaloes beating, & marcht down to yᵉ battoes, & set of about 10 oclock A. M., & passed by the French island we have taken. There was their grand dival & row galley, & our small reddows & prows went with us; we carry none of our heavy artilery nor any of our 13 inch mortars, only the feild peices & royals & sum hoits. When we were got about half way down, sum of our leading boats discovered sum enemy on the shore. Immediately the light infantry row⁴ right to shore & landed against them, but they fled & got clear. When we turnd a point of land near St Johns, we espyed a great smoak at a great distance & one not so large prety nigh us, which proues to be St. Johns, which the enemy have abandon⁴, after seting fire to the fort & buildings;[1] the other is thought to be Shamble,[2] six miles further down the river. We landed & form⁴ without any opposition. This

[1] See Sergeant Holden's Journal of the same date, 2 Proceedings, vol. iv. p. 400.
[2] Probably Fort Chambelle, mentioned by Sergeant Holden, Ibid. See also his Journal under date of September 7, Ibid., p. 401.

place look pleasanter than ye island. Just before night we were ordered to pitch all our tents, & all to lay on our arms with our ammunition all on, being now in our enemys country amongst them where they live. This evening the rangers brought in three prisoners, who informs that they have had a battle 8 days since with Gen! Amherst, but in whose feavour it turnd could not tell. Major Rogers has lost 2 of his men to day & one officer wounded, & the enemy are gone to Montreal; thus Heaven aparantly fights for us, & therefore it is our duty to acknowledge its the hand of Divine Providence, & not done by any force of ours or arm of flesh.

Sunday, 31st August. This morning its loury & rainy, but we are all at work & throwing up intrenchments & forming lines; we have a battery every convenient distance along the lines which, when finish^t, I dont think 10,000 men could force. We have got 16 prisoners [1] this morning. Just now orders came for us to leave off intrenching, as the army is going to march very quick. I then went to see the recruts, where I was well entertained; but what I most prize is, I there found a letter from my brother Jenks, which was to me as cold water to a thirsty soul in this howling & enemys country. To day one of our sloops came down from Isle-aux-Noix, & the row galley taken there & several other boats. We got the cheif of the artelery on shoer. By the best information I can git we took about 60 peices of cannon on the island & sum morters, a great number of shott & shells, & 500 barrells of powder & 100 barrells of pork & 200 of flower, & 30 head of cattle, & other warlike stores. So we may see what is to be depended on about the Frenche not haveing any ammunition or provisions. Had the enemy behaved like men, they could a stood out a month longer, but it plainly appears they are intimidated & Heaven is against them.

Monday, the 1st of September, 1760. This morning we struck our tents at a quarter of an hour after revaloes beating in order to imbarque for Shamble. We did not let off till 3 oclock P. M.; we took up all that time in giting the artelery & camp equippage on board. We then put off & went down, & prety bad falls about a mile long; we got to the place where Rogers took his prisoners last spring, call^d St Thesis, where we stoop^t & incamp^t close by the fort, haveing come about 6 miles from St Johns without any molestation from the enemy. There is a small village of the French here; & their women & children are here, but the men are gone.

Tuseday, 2^d Sep^t, 1760. This morning we are intrenching. Col^o Ingersolls & Col^o Whitcombs regt. are come up; they could not git over the fall last night. I went to view the fort,[2] which was a very

---

[1] Holden says 17. 2 Proceedings, vol. iv. p. 401.
[2] See Sergeant Holden's Journal under date of September 2, Ibid., p. 400.

prety peice of work as any of the French works I have yet seen, but Monseirs have set fire to it since Rogers left it. I hear that 10 of our men drove a 100 French before them & took 5 prisoners & kill^d one ; it plainly appears they are struck with a panick. Just now we are or-dred to leave off intrenching till further orders, for tis supposd we are going to march further. To day, I am ordred to take the pequit at night.

Wednsday, 3^d *Sep*^t, 1760. Last night I lay out with the picquit to keep them alert, now we are in an enemys country. I lay down under the breast work to git a little sleep. I could not help thinking what lodging I have exchanged for this, which is not half so good or convenient as we generally provide for our swine at home ; however, I rested a little. Who would not be a gentleman soldier to lay thus abroad & venture their lives, & when they are at home to be slighted by the generality of mankind. Our rangers keep bringing in the best of the inhabitants, as they take their choice of them ; they also inform us the ladys are very kind in the neighbourhood, which seems we shall fare better when wee git into the thick setled parts of the country. By all I can learn the Indians are all left the French, & will not fight at all, & the inhabitants seem inclined to come in & give up their arms & submit to the Crown of Great Brittain. We are preparing a party to go & take Shamble, which is about 6 miles below us on this river.

Thirsday, 4th *Sep*^t. Last night I had my tent pitcht & fixed so that I lay quite well. This morning about revaloes beating the party going to Shamble set off, consisting of about 1,000 men & several peices of can-non & royals, the whole under the command of Col^o Derby. We are at work at compleating our breastworks, which is almost compleated. The French about here are busy in giting in their harvest, & sum of our men are helping them ; so we are very good neighbours at present. Major Rogers says he heard cannon & plattoons firing yesterday for an hour or two very brisk & smart, so we may expect soon to know the fate of Canada, or our army ; & to day sum of our officers being out to se the village, heard a constant firing of cannon toward Montreal, so would fain hope Genl Murry has got the better of the French, which if he has, we shall soon, I hope, be moueing homeward, for it begins to be cold nights, & our ozuabrig tabernacles is but poor shelter for this cold climate.

Fryday, 5th *Sep*^t, 1760. Last evening we had the agreable news of the surender of the fort at Shamble prisoners of war. There was about 60 French regulars in garison there. Our people took sum of the inhabitants, — women & children, — & placed them before their royall, & so fired over their heads, which answerd instead of faschine bat-terys. After fireing 2 or 3 shells, they hoisted English colours & sub-mited, but wanted the honnors of war, which Col^o Derby would not comply with, threatening them that if they delay[d] any longer he would put all to y[e] sword. We also have news that Gen[l] Murry has had a feild battle with the enemy 3 days agon, near Montreal, & has given Monsiers a worse dressing than they have yet had in America, & there is an express come from Gen[l] Amhers[t], who was got below all the falls, & has good water now all the way to Montreal ; so we are waiting impatiently for news from these armys. About 80 of the French was brought in to camp last night from Shamble. This morning we heard a haavy pcice of cannon fired a defirent way from those we have commonly heard, which is suppos[d] to be the morning gun fired at Gen[l] Amhersts army. We also learn that Mons[r] Levy came over to Laparee[1] with a battallion of regulars, & orders to take the army we had driveing before us, & to assemble the Canadians a this side the river, & give us battle ; but on the aproach of the other army he was ordred back, & the rest we had before us to joyn against Gen[l] Murry, who is able now to give a good account of them, if we are not misinform[d]. O, how aparently does Divine Providence interpose in our feavour ! Altho I bleive if he had come it would a have been to their own cost. God be praised, we are in a condition to receive them. Our men are animated & in high spirits, & fine lines thrown up & redoubts with cannon in front ; & above all, I trust God on our side; therefore we fear them not. Altho an host incamp around us, we will not fear.

Saturday, 6th *September*,[2] 1760. Last evening sum of the militia officers of the French came in, & a party of rangers belonging to Gen[l] Murry. The French came to submit to the Brittish septere, as all have now on the south side of the river St. Lawrence. We have orders to prepare all things to be in readiness to march, I suppose to joyn Gen[l] Murry. I hear this morning that Gen[l] Amherst & Murry joyns armys to day. I am in hopes to see English coulours flying on Montreal yet, for expect soon to march there. To day I have been out about a mile out of camp to git sum blackberrys, & got as many as I could or dare eat. I saw sum of the French women, & they are drest much as those brought from Nova-Scotia. They have sum very prety children as ever I saw any where in my life. I can not find in my heart that I could kill such innocents, altho they have done it many a time on our fronteirs. The country men come in daly with their waggons to carry our provisions & camp equippage to Shamble. This I look on as a forced obedience to us.

Sunday, 7th *Sep[t]*, 1760. This morning have news of Gen[l] Amherst langing on the island of Montreal. We had an express from him last night. There is about a hundred of the French waggons come in this

---

[1] Probably La Prairie.
[2] Birthday of my father's first son, Samuel. — *Note by William Jenks.*

morning to cary our baggage & provisions to Montreal. It looks quite strange to see these Canidians helping our army along to destroy the only place of refuge the miserable creatures have left in their country, which must according to human reason soon fall into our hands.[1] We have got horses to draw our artelery which consists of about 20 as fine brass peices as ever was brought into the feild. There is 60 of the ablest of the invaleads put out to garison Shamble, & the rest we leave here on an island right opposite of our now incampment, under care of Major Emery of the Hamshire troops. The provincials begin to be very sickly. 2 of our battallion died yesterday, & several officers & soldiers are very sick in our reg^t. I desire to bless God I am enabled to go forward with the army, & have not mised 1 tour of duty yet. This afternoon we marched of for Montreal, & got as far as Shamble, & halted a while. The fort look quite beautifull out side. I ded not go in because it was contrary to orders. There is a fine church just below the fort, the first I have seen in this country. There is great numbers of the inhabitants come takeing their oaths of ————, & they are very helpfull in carrying our stores, artellery, & baggege. There is near a 100 waggons of them, & the finest horses for draught that I ever saw in my life any where.

Monday, 8th. Last evening we set out from Shamble, & marcht on through a fine, pleasant country, thick of inhabitants; sum of them look^d very easey & chearfull, others lamenting the fate of their country. Our army marcht in as sevill a manner to the inhabitants as if they had been in our own country. We kept on our march till near midnight in the dark, & waded over 2 rivers & got to an old shed. It rain^d very hard, & we put in here, & I set up all night, for had not room to lay down & got no rest, being wett & very tired. This morning we set out again before sunrise, & it was extreme bad walking occasioned by the rain last night. Our baggege is not come up. I could git no refreshment of no kind, altho never more wanted, I being very ill & weak by a continual flux following this several days. We marched on very fast & waded over another river, & kept on without any sort of sustenance of any kind, vntill about noon, when we arived to a village opposite Montreal, I went into a French house determined to git sum refreshment or stay till the waggons come up. I got sum sower milk, & drank very hearty of it, & then the master of the house came in & asked if we would eat any soup, which I told him we would. They then set before us a fine dish of it; & sum pegions stew^d heads & all on, I here made a fine feast. Had not I met with this nourishment, I could not a held out to march $\frac{1}{4}$ mile further. I then set out for the reg^t, who had got about 2 miles start. We have marcht about 14 miles to day through a fine country for land but not for improve-

[1] See Sergeant Holden's Journal of the same date, 2 Proceedings, vol. iv. p. 401.

ments. We have passed by a great many crosses on the way. Just as I joyn^d the reg^t I saw Col Vaverland [1] put of to go over to Genl Amherst in a whale boat who call^d to shore & told us that the city had surrendred this morning, & that we had done fighting. It seems Gen! Amherst had 3 skirmages with the enemy yesterday & beat them out of their intrenchments. Had they held out a little longer all three of the armys would a laid seige to them, but I desire to bless God we have all Canada now under our command without any more blood shed.[2]

Tuseday, 9th *Sep^t*, 1760. Last night we set up our tents, & I lay very comfortable. Have got such refreshment as made me feel much better. I have joyn^d with Capt Bailey, who tents with me. This morning I got up about an hour by sun, & went to view the city & country. Could see Genl Amhersts camp about 2 miles above the city. This city makes a very beautifull appearance & very fine buildings & beautifull improvements. They look so at a distance. The river is about 2 miles across, & we right opposite the city. I then took a walk after breakfast, with several gen! officers of our battallion down along the river about 4 miles. We went below Gen! Murrys incampment, which is about a mile below the city. Could se great part of the fleet comeing up the river. We went below 1 frigate. This river lies about N. N. E. & S. S. W. & the city lies along by the waters edge & a large mountain on the back. There is no sort of fruit in none of these towns but thorns. They have fine land, but live mesirable to my view. This moment one of Capt Baileys men was found almost dead. Before they could call the docter he died. He had not complaind before, but had eat very freely of pork & cabbage, which kill^d him. This afternoon L, Richardson ariv^d with an express to Gen! Haverland, & brought me three letters, — 1 from my wife, one from brother Sergant, & one from Esqr Goldthwait with the agreable news of their being in health, &c.

Wednsday, 10th *Sept*. Last night I got me a quart of milk & boyl^d it for my supper; then went to cabbin & lay very comfortable till morning, when we had orders to strike our tents, in order to march for Crown point, which was accordingly done, but we did not march till noon, when all the provincials marcht off under com^d of Brigadier Gen! Ruggles. All the regulars stays bhind. It was extreme hot, & we marcht very fast. I thought I could not hold out, but through good Providence I was enabled to stant it till we came to incamp.

Thirsday, 11th *Sep^t*. Last night I lay without any tent, or any thing to cover me with, except a few bushes; & it rain^d very hard in the night, & we were as wet as water could make us. I slept but little. In the morning marcht off for Chamble through very bad way. I got a

---

[1] Gen. Sir William Haviland.

[2] See Sergeant Holden's Journal of the same date, 2 Proceedings, vol. iv. p. 401.

little milk on the way. We ariv^d about noon, & halted here. I found that a Rhod Island officer had taken a tent from my men ; I made application to the field officers for redress, but could get none. I then made a regular complaint to the Brigd^r for the tent, & likewise for satisfaction of him & another officer of same reg^t. Immediately the tent was returnd, tho with regret, & what other satisfaction I am to have I know not yet.

Fryday, 12th *Sep^t*, 1760. Last night lay on the ground without any tent ; a great dew & very cold in the night ; however past the night prety comfortably. I have been in to veiw the fort, which is very neat & beautifully built, tho not strong. I hear one of my men are dead that I left at St Therese, Benj^a Wentworth ; he died the 11th instant. The ladys come very thick to market, — some with one commodity, & sum with other ; however I can not fancy them at no rate. They bring cheifly squashes & turnips & sum cabbage & carrots. I went with a number of gent!men to view the church. We got the sexton & leave to go in ; which was very curious to see their immages & other instrum^{ts} of worship. Returning, went into a French house & got sum bread & milk, which they took no pay for. This part of the country is very pleasant & delightsome. I could fancy to live here had I my partner & friends here. I went in the afternoon to the sutlers, where I saw mankind in their proper hue, when they give a loose to their appetites. To see men, yea such as is stil^d gent^l, git drunk, & then they are stout & must go to fighting.

Saturday, 13th *Sep^t*, 1760. Last night was prety cold. I lay but poorly, & I am in a poor state of health, which dont agree so well together. This morning I went out to git sum breakfast. Return^d ; could git none, which still added to my affliction. This morning our boats ariv^d. I had sum refreshment. About 2 oclock P.M. marched of for St Therese ; arived by sunset, & incampt on the ground we formerly had done. Got sum tea for supper. Id no stomack to eat.

Sunday, 14th *Sept.*, 1760. Last night I lay very comfortable, & slept well. About daybreak struck our tents to imbarque on board battoes for St. Johns. Our men break out very fast with the small pox. I am greatly afraid it will spread in the army, altho al the care we have taken to prevent it. We set off about 8 oclock A.M., wind ahead ; ariv^d at St Johns about noon. Here I got sum refreshment, set off again about 3 oclock P.M. for Isle aux Noix, the wind blowing hard against us, & rough waterr.

Monday, 15th *Sept.*, 1760. Last night got to Ile aux Noix about 8 oclock. I lay on board the boat. About day break I went in to the fort to se after the sick I left behind. Found them all alive. English is very ill ; but took all the sick with me. This fort I will not attempt to discribe for desire it may be erased out of memory for ever, for its not fit for any person to live in, or even to behold. After we had drawn provisions for 4 days to cary us to Crown Point, set of about 9 oclock A.M., the weather rainy & wind ahead. However, we are pressing forward for Crown Point, in hopes to live better & cheaper ; passed by a floating battery built on 2 battoes by the French. We put forward until about sun set, when we went ashore opposite Isle a Mott, haveing come about 30 miles to day. I am sumthing better than I have been this several days. We are cooking all our provisions in order to keep forward without any stop.

Tuseday, 16th *Sep*[t], 1760. Last night I lay very comfortablely. We set off as soon as we could discover any appearance of day. The wind is now favourable at last ; we made as much sail as we could, & to keep in order, which was in 3 colums, 2 battoes a breast. The wind freshen[d] up ; we run at a great rate, the weather prety cold & clear. We kept forward till about 11 oclock at night, when we halted on the east shore about 5 miles from Crown Point, haveing run by computation about ninty miles to day.

Wednsday, 17*th Sep*[t], 1760. Last night I lay very well on board the battoe. We set off this morning about day break, & was obliged to keep in sight of the shore, it being very foggy & cold withal. We ariv[d] about 7 oclock in the morning, & landed & got the sick into the hospital ; went up & was kindly rec[d] by the officers we left behind here. I got a good breakfast, better than I have had since we imbarqed from here. I found M[r] Goldthwait well, who recd me gladly, & informed me he had a line from home, dated 2[d] Sep[t], with news of all being in health.

Thirsday, 18th. To day have been about to see what has been done since we have been gone. It looks as if I had got most home again, haveing come further since I left Montreal than it is to go home from here. To day Esq[r] G. is paying off sum men part of their wages. I wrote 3 letters to send home, — 1 for my girl, 1 for brother John, & 1 for brother Nathan, &c. Directed them to brother Jenks, at Medford. I hear now that Allen Newhall is going home.

Fryday, 19*th Sep*[t], 1760. Last night was very cold. I lay but pooly. This morning Ens[n] Newhall undertook to make us a cabbin to lodg both together in. This day I wrote several letters more to send home, & had a mans things prized by L[t] Knolton, L[t] Foster, Ens[n] Hankerson. They valued them at 7/6 L. M. He died at S[t] Therese. I have been out to walk, in order to git clear of the smell of the camps. I went into the hospital to see the sick, which was a very affecting sight, being about 40 poor creatures.

Saturday, 20th *Sep*[t], 1760. Last night it was reported that the Hamshire [1] and Rhoad Island regiments intended to desert. Immediately a

---

[1] Sergeant Holden refers to this episode under date of the 19th. 2 Proceedings, vol. iv. p. 403

guard of 1 capt., 1 sub, & 60 sergants of the Massachusetts, & sum regulars, to prevent their escape was peraded. They was kept on watch
all night. Those brave fellows did not attempt to desert, but expect they
will soon do it if they are so inclined, & fine character for soldiers. This
morning M! Newhall set off for Lynn by the way of Albany. At evening we came to the former custome of drinking to wives & sweethearts,
& so concluded y° day.

Sunday, 21ˢᵗ, 1760. To day am off duty. I spent most of the day
at L! Burrells house ; it rained for the most part of the day. No sign
of Sunday, except the flags being hoisted. Our chaplains haveing given
us one sermon & prayd 2 or three evenings, which is all we have for
about 20£ L.M., paid by the province per month to chaplains for preach-
ing. A very ill use I think is made of that money ; & 1/8ᵈ cut out of
every doller paid to the soldiers. Who would not fight for such a
court ?

Monday, 22ᵈ *Sept.,* 1760. This mornig I have a 100 men vnder my
care to work in the trench. Carry stones. I am in a poor state of health,
& were I at home I should keep house. To day about 80 battoes set out
for St. Johns to bring Gen! Amherst & sum of his troops that are comeing this way. I have 2 or three men I am afraid have deserted, as I
cannot find them. This day rainy in the forenoon, but pleasant in the
afterpart of the day.

Tuseday, Sep! 23ᵈ. This day am off duty, & I am determined not to
go on again till I am better in health, for a great many officers in camp
have refused that were more able than I am at present. However feel
sumthing better this morning than I did yesterday, & am in hopes to git
well so as not to miss any tour of duty when its my turn. To day I
walked about 5 or 6 miles, in order to keep out of the smell of y° camp.

Wednsday, 24ᵗʰ *Sept.,* 1760. This morning I lay in bed till eight
oclock, being not for duty, & not so bright as I could wish. The most
that is going forward in camp is confining, & holding court martials.
To day its showrey. Just before night L⁴ Richardson arived here from
Isle Noir with several of my men with him. To day Jacob Hasey of
my comp⁷ was taken ill wᵗʰ y° small pox. I hear all the artelery is
just got here. Sum of the Royal Scotch arived her last night from
Lapararee [1] on their way to Hallifax.

Thursday, 25ᵗʰ *Sep!* This day lowery & rainy. I am off duty. In
the morning the Ligoneir & Grand Dival [2] arived from Isle Noir, &
most part of the artelery & several companys of regulars. I & Cap⁴
Hart have bought us a horse [3] that was taken prisoner at Isle Noir, for

---

[1] La Prairie.

[2] Sergeant Holden gives the name " Grand Deoble." 2 Proceedings, vol. iv.
p. 403.

[3] See page 45.

to carry our packs through to N.º 4. I have a cow sum of my men brought me from Isle Noir; they give me her milk till we move from hence. To day Wm. Densmore of my company was carryed to y⁰ hospital, being ill with y' small pox.

Fryday, 26ᵗʰ *Sepᵗ,* 1760. To day am off duty. Joseph Tucker of my company is carryed to the hospital, being ill with the small pox. This is yᵉ 4ᵗʰ I have sick with the small pox, & am afraid it will not be all, for one or 2 more complain. The men in camp begin to die very fast, & its very sickly; there is about 1,200 men of the provincials now returnd unfit for duty, & great many more taken sick almost every day. This eveuing L. R. W. oᵈ: vᵗʰ aˢᵗ ——

Saturday, 27ᵗʰ *Sepᵗ,* 1760. This day is prety pleasant for the season. I went with Capᵗ Hart to find our horse, which we fearᵈ had got lost. After traveling about 2 or 3 miles, found him. To day Corpˡ Bradford of my company came from Ticondaroga, & brings news of Lᵗ Pope being sick, & that Tho! Hoole of my compʸ is dead; but the time when he died he cannot tell. Just before night arived a regiment of Highlanders from Montreal on their way to their winter quarters, which is to be at Hallifax, as I hear.

Sunday, 28ᵗʰ *Sepᵗ,* 1760. This day is very rainy & stormy. I spent most of the day in my tent. In the afternoon went down to yᵉ landing to see the Highland Reg! & the Royall Scotch Reg! embarque for Ticondaroga, & they are to make the best of their way to winter quarters. Our camps be now very sickly; there is not above a third part of the men now in camp that are fit for duty, & there dies more or less every day.

Monday, 29ᵗʰ *Sep!* This day very rainy & cold. I am off duty, & spent most part of the day in tent, for it was exceeding bad walking out, being nothing but mud & water, & very stormy. Joshua Chever has come into our mess. Nathˡ Henderson is come up the lake sick with a flux. Seven men died last night in the provincials, & they will most all die if this weather holds, & they fare no better. I spent most part of the afternoon in Lᵗ Burrills house, as he has a fine fire place.

Tuseday, 30th *Sept.,* 1760. Last night Timothy Townsend of my comp. died in hospital, & this morning was buryed. I have care of 80 men to git the cannon out of the Ligoneir, & hawl up the battoes & boards, that was drove and houe on the shore last night in the storme. About 2 oclock was dismissed. I returnd to camp & made report to the Brigadier of my days work. It now comes on rainy & stormy, & I fear will be bad again to night. About 4 oclock P.M. a gent! brought me a number of letters, wherein I found 4 for me, — 2 from my spouse, one from brother Nathan, & one from brother John, — all dated in Aug!, with the agreable news of their being in health, & a small peice from brother Jenks with news, &c., which is as cold waters to a thirsty

land. After perusing them I went to cabbin ; we lodg well a nights, &
thats all.

Wednsday, the 1ˢᵗ of October, 1760. This day I am off duty; the
weather wett & lowrey. The most part of the day we are obliged to
set in the cabbins with our feet wrapt in our blanketts to keep them
warm ; & here we sett talking & disputing of maters in love & matri-
mony & other diversion to pass away such tedious weather, & to bring
our campeign to an end, as all we have now to do is only fatigue &
nothing to be got nor nothing more to be fought for in America ; so I
don't think any ways out of character to wish an end to our fatigues,
for no honnour is to be got at fatigueing.

Thirsday, 2ᵈ *October*, 1760. To day its sumthing more pleasant than
has been for these several days, altho it looks angry & lowery yet. I
have been out to look for our horse & cow, which were missing; the
latter is found, but the former I fear is lost or stole. I have had several
walks with Capᵗ Hart & Ensn Newball, to find our horse, but they were
all fruitless. Almost all the artelery is got on shore & drawn up on the
bank, which I beleive will be vseless in this country for yᵉ future.

Fryduy, 3 *October*, 1760. The weather is quite pleasant & agreable.
I have been out to walk to find our horse, & found him. Returnd I
heard that Jacob Hasey of my company is dead of the small pox, & one
more not like to live. To day Genˡ Johnson arived here from Montreal,
on his way home. Genˡ Whitmore's regᵗ is arived, & they are to
garison this place this winter.

Saturday, 4ᵗʰ *October*, 1760. To day am off duty. The weather
quite pleasant & warm. I took great satisfaction in walking round the
incampment & fort to see the works. Several vessels came up the
lake. Colᵒ Havaland is arived, & a lord that commands Whitmores
regᵗ I am in hopes that we shall have good weather now, so that the
fort may be got forward before cold weather, that we may git forward
to our province before winter.

Sunday, 5ᵗʰ *October*, 1760. This is a very fine day; I am apt to
think its a weather breeder. I spent most of the day in walking to
take the air & helping Capᵗ Harris, who has been sick aboue a fortnight,
& to day has got out to ride a little in order to git strength. Ater
sunsett we had a sermon preacht on the parade by one of our chaplains from Psalms 63–3. This is the only one I have heard from our
chaplains. He stood 8 minutes by the watch.

Monday, 6ᵗʰ *October*, 1760. Yesterday 3 of my men deserted, viz.,
Wm. Critchett, Benjᵃ Hallowell, & Michal Conoly, & Ebenᵗ Osgood
& Wm. Dinsmore is dead. My company begins to grow small by death
& desertion. I have been out this morning, & there is vast numbers of
pegions flying & geese. To day Joseph Hasey & Jnᵒ Conore arived
here from Isle Noir in a very bad state of health. I fear Hasey will
not recover. This day spent in visiting.

Tusedday, 7ᵗʰ *Octobʳ.*, 1760. To day I am off duty. Fine plesant weather. I went out to walk as usual in order to git a better air than we have in camp, which is almost infectious; such numbers of sick & dead men allways in camp. I hear that the Rhoad Island regᵗ has got the spotted fever amongst them, which is as bad in an army as the plague, as the regular docter says. Great numbers desert every night.

Wednsday, 8ᵗʰ *Octobʳ*, 1760. To day I have care of a party to work in the fort. ░ ░ ░ sey ░ my company died. He is the 7ᵗʰ man I have lost in ░ ░ weeks past, & I fear he is not the last, for have several dangerously sick now. To day the prize row galley came up the lake with men that are discharged, as I hear, as did yᵉ Grand Dioble.[1] To day the sick are mustered, in order to send sum home for New England.

Thirsday, 9ᵗʰ *Octobʳ* ░ ░ rote several letters home, — one ░ ░ I hear several of my men are to ░ ░ home as invaleads. Last night I heard a number of wolues on the other side the lake. To day 2 of Colᵒ Thoˢ men were brought in, haveing deserted, to take the event of their folley.

Frydday, 10 *Octobʳ.*, 1760. This day E ░ att ░ Jathⁿ Winn of my company set off for New England, haveing got their dismission, & Wᵐ Pratt went to help the sick hom . To day I recᵈ a letter from Point Shirley with the confirmation of good news. Ensⁿ Newhall of my company is quite ill. I have taken a great satisfaction to day in walking out without the camp to take the air. I hear Genᶫ Amherst is expected here soon.

Saturday, 11ᵗʰ *October.* To day am off duty. The weather quite agreable & pleasant, which is a great feavour to the sick that set of yesterday in perticular & to the whole army in general. In the afternoon I heard that the putrid fever is brook out at the old fort, & all men are forbid going into it on any account. The evening I went & spent in Capᵗ Baylys tent, where we concluded by drinking to wives.

Sunday, 12ᵗʰ *Octobʳ*, 1760. To day morning great numbers of brants was seen flying over the camp. The weather quite pleasant & agreable. I walked out to gain a good air. Returnᵈ & read over all my letters. Ensⁿ Newhall remains very ill. No regard to sacred time is paid here except a flags flying on yᵉ fort, altho this moment I hear we are to have a sermon, so I must dress to go to meeting, — a rarity up here.

Monday, 13ᵗʰ *Octobʳ*, 1760. To day am off duty. It looks like a storm; I fear a long one. I have taken several walks about to divert myself. Last evening I spent very agreably with Esqʳ Goldthwait, who informᵈ me of Mrs. Hoole's death. I am almost impatiently wishing the arival of Genᶫ Amherst, for I understand that all yᵉ invaleads will be sent home on his arival.

[1] The Dival of 25 September.

Tuseday, 14ᵗʰ *Octoᵇʳ*, 1760. To day it is very rainy. There is no men on fatigue. The weather is so bad I have kept in my tent almost the day in disputeing & other diversions to pass away such dull weather, as its very vncomfortable in camp. I hear a number of letters is come from New England, but cannot find any for me. I hope soon to live without this desire of letters.

Wednsday, 15ᵗʰ *Octoᵇʳ*, 1760. This morning I hear Gen! Amherst is arived, which I find true. Last evening was in very agreable company. To day is cleard up & is fine weather. I am off duty. I spent the day in walking with several gentlemen whose company & conversation was quite agreable. At evening I had sum things prized that blonged to one of my soldiers that is dead, & I assisted other gent¹ on yᵉ like ocasion.

Thirsday, 16ᵗʰ *Octoᵇʳ*, 1760. I hear that all the inveleads are to be sent home immediately, which rejoyces me much, & that we all are to follow in about a fortnight, so hope by God's blessing soon to injoy my friends again in New England. To day I have been settleing about my soldiers things that are dead. I have lost 8 this campeign, but am in great hopes that I shall lose no more, as it now begins to be more healthy in camp.

Fryday, 17th *Octoᵇʳ*, 1760. To day I have care of 112 men to work on fort. I had a smart dispute with the shaif enginoor. To day I saw Mʳ Baldwin from New England. I have had a very pleasant tour of duty to day. I dont expect to have aboue 2 or 3 at furthest more this campeign. I hear there is great numbers of letters on the way; may I have the pleasure of receiveing sum.

Saturday, 18ᵗʰ *Octoᵇʳ*, 1760. To day am off duty. I spent the [day] writeing & walking out round the camp to pass away the time, altho I confess that time is the most precious of all things when a person has the injoyment of his friends company & conversation; altho I have the society of social gentlemen, yet that is not so satisfactory here as else where.

Sunday, 19th *Octoᵇʳ*, 1760. This day is very stormy & cold. I have wrote several letters home & intend them to be the last this campeign without sum extraordinary happens. I spent most all of the day in Capᵗ Bailey's tent reading Milton. Yᵉ evening I spent very agreably with Esqʳ Goldthwait, who tells me he soon intends for New England.

Monday, 20th *Octᵉ*, 1760. To day am off duty. The weather clear, but now begins to be cold. I have been a walk to take the air out of camp. I hear that the invaleads are to be reviewd tomorrow by Docter Monro.¹ No news from home since 23ᵈ Sepᵗ. I heare also that the rangers are to be dismised directly.

¹ Sergeant Holden gives his name "Mun Row." 2 Proceedings, vol. iv. p. 404.

Tuseday, 21ˢᵗ *Octoᵇʳ*, 1760. To day the weather cloudy & cold; likely for snow. I am off duty & have been to see the sick reviewed by Dᵣ Monro, who I think is indued with much more patience than I should have; altho they are my countrymen, yet great numbers of them are a scandall to yᵉ profission of a soldier.

Wednsday, 22ᵈ *Octoᵇʳ*, 1760. Last night it snowᵈ, for this morning the ground looks white, which makes me think of home to git a better house to lodg in than this, which is made of oznabrigs, — a very poor habitation for the inclemency of the season. Ensⁿ Newhall has Dᵣ Monroˑ approbation to go home. I hope soon to follow, for am tired with this campeign.

Thirsday, 23ᵈ *Octoᵇʳ*, 1760. To day am off duty. Its a very cold frosty morning, & the invaleads are prepareing to pass the lake to go home by No. 4,[1] the whole vnder command of Major Gerrish. I bleive the party consists of 500, sum so bad that I think they will never reach New England. There 2 or 3 broke out with the small pox in camp, & it keeps breaking out every full & change of the moon & not above 1 in 3 that has it lives.

Fryday, 24ᵗʰ *Octobʳ*, 1760. To day I have care of a party to work in the fort. I marcht them into the fort & stayᵈ a while, but found my self so ill that I could not stand it. I gave charge of the party to 2 subbs that was with me & returnd to camp. I fear I am going to have a fit of sickness, for am very bad seized with a cold. To day Enˑ Newhall set out for home.

Saturday, 25th *Octoᵇʳ*, 1760. This morning, blessed be God, I find myself much better. I hope it will go off without a setled fever, which I much fearᵈ yesterday. I have returnᵈ my self sick, the only time I have been returnd so this campeign. I am not very zealous now for duty time. I think we ought to be dismised to git home before winter.

Sunday, 26ᵗʰ *Octobʳ*, 1760. This day I am sum better, but not so well as to be fit for duty. Esqʳ Goldthwait I hear has recᵈ instructions from home to [stay] till the camp breaks up, so am like to have his company a while longer. I can hear no news at all from home. It seems they have forgot me.

Monday, 27ᵗʰ *Octobʳ*, 1760. This day we have built us a chimney to our tent, for we can no longer stand to live without a fire. To day Genˡ Amherst set off for Albany, & now I fear we shall be kept till yᵉ last of November, for yᵉ command is left to Haverland, & I know he delights to fatigue yᵉ provincials.

Tuseday, 28ᵗʰ *Octobʳ*, 1760. To day am much better of my cold. The weather now looks winter like, & it is constantly snowing on the

---

[1] See note, 2 Proceedings, vol. iv. p. 404.

mountains to the N. W. of us. I spend most of my time in gossopping from one neighbour to another to pass away the tedious hours till we can be set at liberty, &c.

Wednesday, 29th *Octo*^{br}, 1760. This is a pleasant, altho a frosty morning. Our lads has been bringing a house for them to cook in. Can see the snow on the mountains. Looks as if it wer 3 or 4 feet deep. I beleive we shall soon have a share of snow here, for it has got to be a nigh neighbour.

Thirsday, 30th *Octo*^r, 1760. To day prety pleasant for the season. Col? Thomas is arived from Isle Noir, after demolishing all the works & fortifications on that almost infernal island. I pray it may never have any inhabants on there any more forever, without its owls & satyrs or dragons of the deserts, but be bloted out of memory to all ages.

Fryday, 31st *Oct*.^r, 1760. To day its very pleasant weather, & the commanding officer keeps all the troops on fatigue, so eager are they to git all they possibly can out of us before they dismis us. I think this parallell with ye devils rage, when he knew his time was short to plague mankind in; so I know their time is short like their masters. To day Esqr Goldthwait set off for Albany.

Saturday, 1^a *November*, 1760. Last evening I saw Phineas Douglas, & he tells me his brother Joseph is gone home lame, & that his friends was all well lately. To day I have care of 100 men to work in the fort; the weather blustring & cold. I kept with the party about half ye day, & the other officers the rest. At evening it rain^d prety much.

Sunday, 2^d *Nov*^m, 1760. This morning the weather quite clear & pleasant. I understand that we shall tarry till ye 20th instant, without we should git the barracks done before, & that we shall all be gone off by then whether they are done or not. To day I spent in my tent in reading & writeing. No sign at all of Sunday now, for the flag is not hoisted at all.

Monday, 3^d *Nov*^m, 1760. To day the weather pleasant for the season; can see the tops of the mountains all covered with snow all round. I beleive we are in a warm climate compared with those mountains. I have been all round the fort twice to see how the barrack goes on. I am in hopes they will be done by ye 10th or 12th of this month; so hope to have our freedom again in short time.

Tuseday, 4th *November*, 1760. To day am off duty; the weather pleasant for the season. To day Col^o Hawk & a party with him set out for N? 4; they are to make a bridge over Otter Creek. I hear Major Gerrish got through to No 4 with the loss of but one or 2 of his party. The party of 80 sent by Major Hobble to Albany, I hear 70 of them are dead ; & another small party sent that way since, I hear 18 of them are gone the way of all flesh. So frail a creature is man !

Wednsday, 5th November, 1760, *Powder Plot.* This day all the carpenters that can work on the barrocks was ordred to assist those already on that work ; & the masons will have done their barrock fit for the carpenters in 2 days more. I have been round the fort to see the works, and they go on quite briskly, for the provincials are of the mind that we shall be discharg'd as soon as the barrocks are covered ; so by that rule we shall march for home by the 10th or 12th instant.

Thirsday, 6th November, 1760. Last evening the provincials, as it was Pope Night, kept fireing all over the camps. Altho all possible care was taken to detect them & suppress the fire, yet they kept a constant fireing & squibing in defirent parts of the incampments till bed time. This day I am off duty ; the weather quite warm for the season. Have had several walks round the fort to see the works, & they will be so far compleated as to admit of our dismission in about a week at furthest.

Fryday, 7th November, 1760. To day I am on duty at drawing timber into the fort. I had a task which I finished before noon ; this is the only task I have had on the works this campeign. In the afternoon I spent my time very agreably in walking out with several gentlemen to git a better air than can be injoyd in camp. Last night 2 of Cap' Butterfields men died suddenly.

Saturday, 8th November, 1760. This morning rainy & lowry ; looks quite like for bad weather, which has kept off for a great while. However, the working party kept at work till night. To day the brigg was sent to Ticondaroga to be hawled up for to winter. The camp ladys now, like the swallows, are seeking a more convenient climate to winter in, for they are packing off.

Sunday, 9th Novm., 1760. To day exceeding stormy, haveing rain'd & snowd all night. I lay a bed till ten oclock. In the afternoon returned all my arms into the ship stores, as its orders for the first & second battell, to return all their arms in. I hope now soon to be on my march for home, for certainly they dont intend us for any more fighting. Just at night it cleard up, but too late for the working party to turn out.

Monday, 10th Nov^m, 1760. To day the weather quite pleasant, considering the climate & season. To day Rufus Hayward of my company was carry'd to the hospitall sick with the small pox ; I fear it will go hard with him. To day I gave warrents to sum of my serjants to clear them from the melitious officers at home, for I think to good to be hawl'd out by them.

Tuseday, 11th Nov^r, 1760. To day am off duty. The weather cold & churlish. Last night John Connore of my company died in the hospitall; he is the 10th man I have lost, & I fear that is not all. We continue working on the fort & barracks to compleat them, so that the troops that winter here may be comfortable.

Wednsday, y 12th Nov^r, 1760.* To day a large party of invaleads was sent home by No. 4, under the care of Col? Whitcomb; & another party that are not able to go by No. 4, is going by Albany under the care of Col° Saltonstall, so that we shall not have any sick left in camp I hope when these are gone.

Thirsday, 13th November, 1760. To day I have care of 100 men in drawing up the cannon brought from y° Island Noir, & drew up 33 before the working partys left off. To day Col? Saltonstall set out with his party of sick for Albany. The weather is very cold, & looks now like snow; its the coldest day we have had this fall.

Fryday, 14th Nov^m, 1760. Last night it snowd best part of the night, & this morning the snow is about 6 inches deep on a levell, & extreame cold & windey. Yet our good friends the regulars turnd out the proveutials on fatigue sooner than usual, & kept their own men off of the works. To day Capt Hart & my self had our horse shod, & frowed to cary our packs to No. 4.

Saturday, 15th November, 1760. Last night was an extreame cold one; however I lay comfortably, considering I had no covering for a house but a Oznbrigg tabernakle. To day there is no drum beat for the works, & we have orders to make a return of all invaleads able & unable for march, & I beleive that we shall soon be on our march for the pumkin country. I almost dread our passage to No. 4; its about a 100 miles & now its bad traveling. To day Capt Bayley was carried to the hospitall, being ill with the small pox, & Lt Putnam is ille of y° same.

Sunday, 16th Nov^m, 1760. To day Capt Page of our batt^{ll} was sent off with a party of 60 well men to No. 4. Yesterday a stage on the barrock gave way, by which means 3 men fell from the roof that were shingleing, & hurt themselves so much that their lives are dispaired of. To day a party of provincials was sent to Ticondaroga for provisions. After we haue work^d on the fort till y° cold drove us off, now we have provisions to bring here for all the garisson, under y° pretence of bringing it for us to carry us to No. 4. I perceive that its Sunday to day, for y° flag is flying. I hear this morning that several of the regulars cows are dead, — froze to death last night; but I had rather think sum of our rouges helped them because they are almost outragious at being kept here in camp at this season. I heard that Col? Haverland, going round the fort, fell down & broke his leg. Poor man! I am sorry it was his leg. To day orders came for all the tools to [be] return^d in, & all the arteficers to be paid off tomorrow.

Monday, 17ᵗʰ *November,* 1760. To day a party was sent up to Ticondaroga with our baker to bake bread to carry us to No 4, our oven here being fell in & rendred useless. In the afternoon we had orders to march to Ticondaroga, & take 8 days provisions to cary us to No. 4. The weather is so bad that the carpenters cannot work, or we should tarry 3 days longer.

Tuseday, 18*th Novᵐ.,* 1760. This morning about day break we struck our tents & dliverd them in, & march off about 8 oclock A. M. I am rejoyced to be on a march again. We arived at Ticondaroga about 3 oclock P. M., and were till 10 oclock at night gitting over the lake. The weather tedious cold. I have a bad pain in my right knee that I can hardly march with yᵉ regiment.

Wednsday, 19*th Novᵐ,* 1760. This morning we tarry here waiting for our bread to be baked. The weather extreame cold. I lay very comfortably by a large fire without any hut or tent, & now it looks homish, as the man said by his barn, altho we are but just seting out. My knee so lame, I fear I shall have a bad time through yᵉ woods, but desire to put my trust in Him that can do all things according to his pleasure, & go as well & far as I can. Set off about 10 oclock, & marcht till about 3 oclock & campt.

Thirsday, 20*th Novᵐ.,* 1760. Last night lay very well by a large fire; the weather extream cold, & the way exceeding bad. We have come about 14 miles. We marcht off this morning about sunrise, & march on through extreame bad way about 15 miles, & passd by a man left on the road burnt by falling in the fire. He was left with 2 others to take care of, who, when the poor creature fell into a sleep, took all the provisions & marcht of & left him, first covering him over with hemlock boughs, & reported that he was dead, & they had buried him. These villians were whipt — one 500 lashes, yᵉ other 250 — for their inhumanity, by order of a court martial @ No 4.

Fryday, 21ˢᵗ *Novᵐ,* 1760. Last night lay by a fire; it snowd sum in the night. Set off this morning by day, & marcht on in exceeding bad way & came to Otter Creek, & campt just by a wolfe killd by sum of our men & laid by the way.

Saturday, 22ᵈ *Novʳ.,* 1760. Set of early, & past Otter Creek, & kept on over the height of land. Met Col Whitcomb & several horses going for sum sick.

Sunday, 23ᵈ *Novᵐ,* 1760. Set off early throug vast mountains, & went over sum reacht almost to the clouds, & got into the road hard by yᵉ Hamshire troops.

Monday, 24*th Novᵐ.,* 1760. Set off about 4 oclock. Raind steady all day. Have 16 mile to N° 4.

Tuseday, 25th Nov™, 1760. Continued at No 4. Mustred my men & sent them off. To day 2 provincial was whipt for ———— [1]

Wednsday, 26 Nov™, 1760. I waited here last night for Cap* Hart, &c. Set off about 7 oclock **A. M.** Have now none to take care off but my self, as all my company are dismissed & gone home before me.

NOTES.

[Three pages in the handwriting of Rev. William Jenks, D.D., son of the Diarist.]

Smollett, vol. 5, p. 276, says General Amherst "detached Colonel Haviland, with a body of troops from Crown Point, to take possession of the Isle aux Noix, in the Lake Champlain, & from thence penetrate the shortest way to the bank of the River St Lawrence." He had before directed Gen. Murray to advance from Quebec to Montreal, & now proceeded "with the main body of the army, amounting to about 10,000 men, including Indians," from Albany to Lake Ontario & down the S. Lawrence. Col. Sewall observes that the junction of the forces about Montreal was, in his opinion, by no means unforeseen or unintentional, for on the march Col. Haviland's corps was occasionally hastened and retarded; though Smollett says expressly, "they had no intelligence of the motions of each other."

"On the 6th day of Sept. Gen. Amherst's troops were landed on the island of Montreal," & after marching so lay all night on their arms before the city. Next day a letter was sent by the Marquis de Vaudreuil demanding a capitulation, which was granted. " General Murray, with the troops from Quebec, had by this time landed on the island; & Col. Haviland, with the body under his command, had just arrived on the south side of the river opposite to Montreal, — circumstances," adds Smollett, "equally favourable & surprising."

Col. Sewall observes that Gen. Haviland had sent the baggage, tents, &c., up the Sorel after they were remanded back; so that the provincial troops on their return were exposed, as in this journal is related,

[1] Sergeant Holden's Journal supplies the blank under the same date. "Two men that was Confin'd for Burying a man alive in N° 4 woods Rec'd their punishment, one Rec'd 500 Lashes, the other 100." Though perhaps there is some confusion of dates, and his reference is to the incident above under date of November 20. 2 Proceedings, vol. iv. p. 400.

to the cold & rain at night; that as orders had arrived forbidding any of Col. Haviland's troops to visit the city, Brig. Ruggles was greatly dissatisfied, & hurried on his men in such manner that, being compelled to lodge in the open air, exposed to the heavy rain, they fell sick ; & from being a healthy army, with but very few unable to do duty, they returned a weakly, diseased body, with hardly a third of them serviceable, & "began to die away like rotten sheep."

Smollett terms the conquest of Canada "the most important of any the British arms ever achieved," & says, "The zeal & conduct of Brigadier General Gage, the undaunted spirit & enterprising genius of General Murray, the diligence & activity of Colonel Haviland, happily co-operated in promoting this great event." For he observes it must be allowed Gen. Amherst "was extremely fortunate in having subordinate commanders who perfectly corresponded with his ideas, & a body of troops whom no labours could discourage, whom no dangers could dismay."

Gen. Amherst's whole conduct was irreproachable, & Sir Wm. Johnson had influence over the Indians to restrain them from every atrocity. (p. 281, &c.)

BATH, Mar. 29, 1811

[Then follow 126 blank pages and the seven pages on which are these entries in pencil, as if some one had intended to use the book for a diary or journal, and then gave up the idea.]

Satterday, September. I re hemed Mr Batta 3 handkerchief, one of our boarders.

Friday.

Thirsday.

Wednesday.

Tuesday.

Monday.

Sunday.

[A number of pages of miscellaneous memoranda follow.]

1766, *Febry* 12th. The river was open, & the first boat went down then; it was B. Hall's.

Febry 20th. Died the Widow Tyler, & was carried to Boston to be buried.

March 29. @ half after two o'clock in the morning was born my son Saml, of a Saturday.

Sunday, 30 March. Died Mr. Kidder, very suddenly; was well at ten A. M., & dead by the time the first bell rung for the afternoon service.

Sunday, 6 April. Died Mrs. Bradshaw, wife of Dea^c Jon^t Bradshaw, of a lingering disease, haveing been deprivd of her reason for a long time.

[A memorandum of things from Jan. 1, 1766.]

Wednesday, ye 8th *Jan^y.* Was married Henry Fowle to Mary Patten.

Wednesday, 15th. Then Mr. Hez^h Blanchard took out Draper's news paper for himself & me; he paid 12/6 old ten, & I 12/6, being ye $\frac{1}{2}$.

Wednesday, 22^d January. Was married John Wade & Betty Pool.

Febry 6, Thursday. Was maried Mr Charles Pelham & Molley Tyler.

Pd Critchett 1 dollar for 1 share in a horse. Pd 2/ to another for a share in do. Capt Hart gave a q^{rt} brandy for 1 do. in do. Sept. 25, 1760.

Lent Benjn Hallowell 1 dollr, Sep^t 25th, 1760.

Tuseday, 26th Aug, 1760. Then Corp! Ephraim Rhoads was broke & reduced to do duty of a private by a court martial. Done at camp before Ile aux Noix.

Bought 3 galls rum & 9 ℔ sug^r, 1 bottle wine.

Ens^n Newhall bought 15 ℔ sug^r & 1 bottle wine.

Ens^n Newhall Dr.

Augt., 1760		Yorke currency
7th	To cash lent him	0 – 5

Crown Point, 23^d July.

Lent Lt Richardson 20 ℔ sug^r @ 1/4	1 –	6 – 8
do 6 ℔ chocolate @ 4/–	1 – 4	
do 6 ℔ coffe @ 2/6 —	0 – 15	
do 1 cheese, wt 16 gr, @ 1/8	1 –	9 – 6

Lent Capt Hart 4 ℔ coffee.

Borrowd of do. 20 ℔ sug^r & 6 ℔ coffee

Ballanced.

[A pen mark is run through this entry.]

Lent Mr. Hobby 2 ℔ cheese.

Cr. to Lt Richardson to 25 ℔ soap.

Augt. 1760

27th Ezra Pratt to 12^r vinegar.

Crown Point, 23^d July, 1760. } Yorke
Bought of Mr Neagle, setler. } currency.

one cheese, w^d 16½ @ 1/8	£1 – 7 – 6
& 3 ℔ tobacco @ 2/	0 – 6
1 pr shoes 15/	0 – 15
1 pr buck ells 2/	0 – 2
25th 50 ℔ chocolate @ 3/3	8 – 2 – 6
1 pr pumps 15/–	0 – 15
to 158 ℔ sugar @ 1/3^d	9 – 17 – 6
81½ ℔ cheese @ 1/8	6 – 5 – 10
27th 1 pr shoes 15/	0 – 15
1 ℔ soap 1/6	0 – 1 – 6
	28 – 7 – 10

www.ingramcontent.com/pod-product-compliance
Lightning Source LLC
Chambersburg PA
CBHW032135080426
42733CB00008B/1083